With the Tanks

With the Tanks

Two first-hand accounts of
British Tanks & Tank-men at war
in Europe during the First World War

Life in a Tank
Richard Haigh

Men and Tanks
J. C. MacIntosh

LEONAUR

With the Tanks
Two first-hand accounts of
British Tanks & Tank-men at war
in Europe during the First World War
Life in a Tank by Richard Haigh
Men and Tanks by J. C. MacIntosh

First published under the titles
Life in a Tank
and
Men and Tanks

Leonaur is an imprint of Oakpast Ltd

Copyright in this form © 2009 Oakpast Ltd

ISBN: 978-1-84677-978-7 (hardcover)
ISBN: 978-1-84677-977-0 (softcover)

http://www.leonaur.com

Publisher's Notes

In the interests of authenticity, the spellings, grammar and place names used have been retained from the original editions.

The opinions of the authors represent a view of events in which he was a participant related from his own perspective, as such the text is relevant as an historical document.

The views expressed in this book are not necessarily those of the publisher.

A TANK ON ITS WAY INTO ACTION

Life in a Tank

Richard Haigh

Contents

Contents

CHAPTER 1

The Meaning of the Tank Corps

Tanks!

To the uninitiated—as were we in those days when we returned to the Somme, too late to see the tanks make their first
dramatic entrance—the name conjures up a picture of an iron
monster, breathing fire and exhaling bullets and shells, hurling
itself against the enemy, unassailable by man and impervious to
the most deadly engines of war; sublime, indeed, in its expression of indomitable power and resolution.

This picture was one of the two factors which attracted us
toward the Heavy Branch Machine-Gun Corps—as the Tank
Corps was known in the first year of its being. On the Somme
we had seen a derelict tank, wrecked, despoiled of her guns,
and forsaken in No Man's Land. We had swarmed around and
over her, wild with curiosity, much as the Lilliputians must have
swarmed around the prostrate Gulliver. Our imagination was
fired.

The second factor was, frankly, that we were tired of going
over the top as infantrymen. The first time that a man goes into
an attack, he as a rule enjoys it. He has no conception of its
horrors,—no, not horrors, for war possesses no horrors,—but,
rather, he has no knowledge of the sudden realization of the
sweetness of life that comes to a man when he is "up against it."
The first time, it is a splendid, ennobling novelty. And as for the
"show" itself, in actual practice it is more like a dream which
only clarifies several days later, after it is all over. But to do the

same thing a second and third and fourth time, is to bring a man face to face with Death in its fullest and most realistic uncertainty. In soldier jargon he "gets most awful wind up."

It is five minutes before "Zero Hour." All preparations are complete. You are waiting for the signal to hop over the parapet. Very probably the Boche knows that you are coming, and is already skimming the sandbags with his machine guns and knocking little pieces of earth and stone into your face. Extraordinary, how maddening is the sting of these harmless little pebbles and bits of dirt! The bullets ricochet away with a peculiar singing hiss, or crack overhead when they go too high. The shells which burst on the other side of the parapet shake the ground with a dull thud and crash.

There are two minutes to wait before going over. Then is the time when a man feels a sinking sensation in his stomach; when his hands tremble ever so slightly, and when he offers up a pathetic little prayer to God that if he's a bit of a sportsman he may be spared from death, should his getting through not violate the divine and fatalistic plans. He has that unpleasant lack of knowledge of what comes beyond. For after all, with the most intense belief in the world, it is hard to reconcile the comforting feeling of what one knows with that terrible dread of the unknown.

A man has no great and glorious ideas that nothing matters because he is ready to die for his country. He is, of course, ready to die for her. But he does not think about it. He lights a cigarette and tries to be nonchalant, for he knows that his men are watching him, and it is his duty to keep up a front for their sake. Probably, at the same time, they are keeping up a front for him. Then the sergeant major comes along, cool and smiling, as if he were out for a stroll at home. Suddenly he is an immense comfort. One forgets that sinking feeling in the stomach and thinks, "How easy and jolly he is! What a splendid fellow!" Immediately, one begins unconsciously to imitate him. Then another thinks the same thing about one, and begins to imitate too. So it passes on, down the line. But there is nothing heroic or exalting in going over the top.

12

This, then, was our possible second reason for preferring to attack inside bullet-proof steel; not that death is less likely in a tank, but there seems to be a more sporting chance with a shell than with a bullet. The enemy infantryman looks along his sight and he has you for a certainty, but the gunner cannot be so accurate and twenty yards may mean a world of difference. Above all, the new monster had our imaginations in thrall. Here were novelty and wonderful developments.

In the end of 1916, therefore, a certain number of officers and men received their orders to join the H.B.M.G.C., and proceeded sorrowfully and joyfully away from the trenches. Sorrowfully, because it is a poor thing to leave your men and your friends in danger, and get out of it yourself into something new and fresh; joyfully, because one is, after all, but human.

About thirty miles behind the line some villages were set aside for the housing and training of the new units. Each unit had a nucleus of men who had already served in tanks, with the new arrivals spread around to make up to strength.

The new arrivals came from all branches of the Service; Infantry, Sappers, Gunners, Cavalry, and the Army Service Corps. Each man was very proud of his own Branch; and a wonderfully, healthy rivalry and affection sprang up between them. The gunner twitted the sapper, the cavalryman made jokes at the A.S.C., and the infantryman groused at the whole lot. But all knew at the bottom of their hearts, how each is essential to the other.

It was to be expected when all these varied men came together, that the inculcating of a proper *esprit de corps*—the training of each individual in an entirely new science for the benefit of the whole—would prove a very difficult and painstaking task. But the wonderful development, however, in a few months, of a large, heterogeneous collection of men into a solid, keen, self-sacrificing unit, was but another instance of the way in which war improves the character and temperament of man.

It was entirely new for men who were formerly in a regiment, full of traditions, to find themselves in the Tank Corps. Here was a Corps, the functions of which resulted from an idea born of the exigencies of this science-demanding war. Unlike every other branch of the Service, it has no regimental history to direct it, no traditions upon which to build, and still more important from a practical point of view, no experience from which to draw for guidance, either in training or in action.

In the Infantry, the attack has resulted from a steady development in ideas and tactics, with past wars to give a foundation and this present one to suggest changes and to bring about remedies for the defects which crop up daily. With this new weapon, which was launched on the Somme on September 15, 1916, the tactics had to be decided upon with no realistic experimentation as ground work; and, moreover, with the very difficult task of working in concert with other arms of the Service that had had two years of fighting, from which to learn wisdom.

With regard to discipline, too,—of all things the most important, for the success of a battle has depended, does, and always will depend, upon the state of discipline of the troops engaged,—all old regiments have their staff of regular instructors to drill and teach recruits. In them has grown up that certain feeling and loyalty which time and past deeds have done so much to foster and cherish. Here were we, lacking traditions, history, and experience of any kind.

It is easy to realize the responsibility that lay not only upon the chief of this new corps, but upon each individual and lowest member thereof. It was for us all to produce *esprit de corps*, and to produce it quickly. It was necessary for us to develop a love of the work, not because we felt it was worthwhile, but because we knew that success or failure depended on each man's individual efforts.

But, naturally, the real impetus came from the top, and no admiration or praise can be worthy of that small number of men in whose hands the real destinies of this new formation lay; who were continually devising new schemes and ideas for binding the whole together, and for turning that whole into a highly efficient, up-to-date machine.

"How did the tank happen to be invented?" is a common

King George and Queen Mary inspecting a tank on the British front in France

question. The answer is that in past wars experience has made it an axiom that the defenders suffer more casualties than the attacking forces. From the first days of 1914, however, this condition was reversed, and whole waves of attacking troops were mown down by two or three machine guns, each manned, possibly, by not more than three men.

There may be in a certain sector, before an attack, an enormous preliminary bombardment which is destined to knock out guns, observation posts, dumps, men, and above all, machine-gun emplacements. Nevertheless, it has been found in actual practice that despite the most careful observation and equally careful study of aeroplane photographs, there are, as a rule, just one or two machine guns which, either through bad luck or through precautions on the part of the enemy, have escaped destruction. These are the guns which inflict the damage when the infantrymen go over and which may hold up a whole attack.

It was thought, therefore, that a machine might be devised which would cross shell-craters, wire and trenches, and be at the same time impervious to bullets, and which would contain a certain number of guns to be used for knocking out such machine guns as were still in use, or to lay low the enemy infantry.

With this idea, a group of men, in the end of 1915, devised the present type of heavy armoured car. In order to keep the whole plan as secret as possible, about twenty-five square miles of ground in Great Britain were set aside and surrounded with armed guards. There, through all the spring and early summer of 1916, the work was carried on, without the slightest hint of its existence reaching the outside world. Then, one night, the tanks were loaded up and shipped over to France, to make that first sensational appearance on the Somme, with the success which warranted their further production on a larger and more ambitious scale.

CHAPTER 2

First Days of Training

We were at a rest camp on the Somme when the chit first came round regarding the joining of the H.B.M.G.C. The colonel came up to us one day with some papers in his hand.

"Does anybody want to join this?" He asked.

We all crowded around to find out what "this" might be.

"Tanks!" someone cried. Some were facetious; others indifferent; a few mildly interested. But no one seemed very keen about it, especially as the tanks in those days had a reputation for rather heavy casualties. Only Talbot, remembering the derelict and the interest she had inspired, said, with a laugh,—

"I rather think I'll put my name down, sir. Nothing will come of it, but one might just as well try." And taking one of the papers he filled it in, while the others stood around making all the remarks appropriate to such an occasion.

Two or three weeks went by and Talbot had forgotten all about it, in the more absorbing events which crowded months into days on the Somme.

One day the adjutant came up to him and, smiling, put out his hand.

"Well, goodbye, Talbot. Good luck."

When a man puts out his hand and says "Goodbye," you naturally take the proffered hand and say "Goodbye," too. Talbot found himself saying "Goodbye" before he realized what he was doing. Then he laughed.

"Now that I've said 'Goodbye, where am I going?" he asked.

"To the Tanks," the adjutant replied.

So he was really to go; really to leave behind his battalion, his friends, his men, and his servant. For a moment the Somme and the camp seemed the most desirable places on earth. He thought he must have been a fool the day he signed that paper signifying his desire to join another corps. But it was done now. There were his orders in the colonel's hand.

"When do I start, sir? And where do I go?" he asked.

"You're to leave immediately for B——, wherever that is. Take your horse as far as the railhead and get a train for B——, where the Tank Headquarters are. Goodbye, Talbot; I'm sorry to lose you." A silent handshake, and they parted.

Talbot's kit was packed and sent off on the transport. A few minutes later he was shaking hands all round. His spirits were rising at the thought of this new adventure, but it was a wrench, leaving his regiment. It was, in a way, he thought, as if he were turning his back on an old friend. The face of Dobbin, his groom, as he brought the horses round was not conducive to cheer. He must get the business over and be off. So he mounted and rode off through a gray, murky drizzle, to the railhead about eight miles away. There came the parting with Dobbin and with his pony. Horses mean as much as men sometimes, and his had worked so nobly with him through the mud on the Somme. He wondered if there would be any one in the new place who would be so faithful to him as Polly. Finally, there was Dobbin riding away, back to M——, with the horse, and its empty saddle, trotting along beside him. It was simply rotten leaving them all!

One has, however, little time for introspection in the army, and especially when one engages in a tilt with an R.T.O. The R.T.O. has been glorified by an imaginative soul with the title of "Royal Transportation Officer." As a matter of fact, the "R" does not stand for "royal," but for "railway," and the "T" is "transport," nothing so grandiose as "transportation." Now an R.T.O.'s job, though it may be a safe one, is not enviable. He is forced to combine the qualities of booking-clerk, station-master, goods-agent, information clerk, and day and night watchman all into one. In consequence of this it is necessary for the traveller's speech and attitude to be strictly soothing and complimentary. Talbot's obsession at this moment was as to whether B—— was near or far back from the line.

If he supposed that B—— was "near" the line, the R.T.O. might tell him just to prove how kind Fate is that it was a good many miles in the rear. But no such luck. The R.T.O. coldly informed Talbot that he hadn't the slightest idea where B—— was. He only knew that trains went there. And, by the way, the trains didn't go there direct. It would be necessary for him to change at Boulogne. Talbot noticed these signs of thawing with delight. And to change at Boulogne! Life was brighter.

Travelling in France in the northern area, at the present time, would seem to be a refutation of the truth that a straight line is the shortest distance between two points. For in order to arrive at one's destination, it is usually necessary to go about sixty miles out of one's way,—hence the necessity for Talbot's going to Boulogne in order to get a train running north.

He arrived at Boulogne only to find that the train for B—— left in an hour.

He strolled out into the streets. Boulogne had then become the Mecca for all those in search of gaiety. Here were civilized people once again. And a restaurant with linen and silver and shining glass, and the best dinner he had ever eaten.

When he had paid his bill and gone out, he stopped at the corner of the street just to look at the people passing by. A large part of the monotony of this war is occasioned, of course, by the fact that the soldier sees nothing but the everlasting drab of uniforms. When a man is in the front line, or just behind, for weeks at a time he sees nothing but soldiers, soldiers, soldiers! Each man has the same coloured uniform; each has the same pattern tunic, the same puttees. Each is covered with the same mud for days at a time. It is the occasion for a thrill when a "Brass Hat" arrives, for he at least has the little brilliant red tabs on his tunic! A man sometimes finds himself envying the soldiers of the old days who could have occasional glimpses of the dashing uniforms of their officers, and although a red coat makes a target of a man, the colour is at least more cheerful than the eternal khaki. The old-time soldier had his red coat and his bands, blaring encouragingly. The soldier of today has his drab and no music at all, unless he sings. And every man in an army is not gifted with a voice.

So Talbot looked with joy on the charming dresses and still more charming faces of the women and girls who passed him. Even the men in their civilian clothes were good to look upon.

Riding on French trains is very soothing unless one is in a hurry. But unlike a man in civil life, the soldier has no interest in the speed of trains. The civilian takes it as a personal affront if his train is a few minutes late, or if it does not go as fast as he thinks it should. But the soldier can afford to let the Government look after such minor details. The train moved along at a leisurely pace through the lovely French countryside, making frequent friendly stops at wayside stations. On the platform at Etaples station was posted a rhyme which read:

A wise old owl lived in an oak,
The more he saw, the less he spoke;
The less he spoke, the more he heard;
Soldiers should imitate that old bird.

It was the first time that Talbot had seen this warlike ditty. Its intention was to guard soldiers from saying too much in front of strangers. Talbot vowed, however, to apply its moral to himself at all times and under all conditions.

From nine in the morning until half-past two in the afternoon they rolled along, and had covered by this time the extraordinary distance of about forty miles! Here at last was the station of Saint-P——.

Talbot looked about him. Standing near was an officer with the Machine-Gun Corps Badge, whom he hailed, and questioned about the Headquarters of the Tank Corps.

"About ten miles from here. Are you going there?" the fellow

20

asked.

Talbot explained that he hoped to, and being saturated with Infantry ideas, he wondered if a passing motor lorry might give him a lift.

The man laughed. "Why don't you telephone Headquarters and ask them to send a car over for you?" he asked.

Talbot did not quite know whether the fellow were ragging him or not. He decided that he was, for who had ever heard of "telephoning for a car"?

"Oh, I don't believe I'll do that—thanks very much for the hint, all the same," he said. "Just tell me which road to take and I'll be quite all right."

The officer smiled.

"I'm quite serious about it," he said. "We all telephone for cars when we need them. There's really no point in your walking—in fact, they'll be surprised if you stroll in upon them. Try telephoning and you'll find they won't die of shock."

Partly to see whether they would or not, and partly because he found the prospect of a motorcar more agreeable than a ten-mile walk, Talbot telephoned. Here he experienced another pleasant surprise, for he was put through to Headquarters with no difficulty at all. A cheerful voice answered and he stated his case.

"Cheero," the voice replied. "We'll have a car there for you in an hour—haven't one now, but there will be one ready shortly."

Saint-P—— was a typical French town, and Talbot strolled around. There were soldiers everywhere, but the town had never seen the Germans, and it was a pleasant place. There was, too, a refreshing lack of thick mud—at least it was not a foot deep.

Although Talbot could not quite believe that the car would materialize, it proved to be a substantial fact in the form of a box-body, and in about an hour he was speeding toward Headquarters. It was dark when they reached the village, and as they entered, he experienced that curious feeling of apprehensive expectancy with which one approaches the spot where one is to live and work for some time to come. The car slowed up to pass some carts on the road, and started forward with such a jerk that Talbot was precipitated from the back of the machine into the road. He picked himself up, covered with mud. The solemn face of the driver did not lessen his discomfiture. Here was a strange village, strange men, and he was covered with mud!

Making himself as presentable as possible, Talbot reported to Headquarters, and was posted to "J" Company, 4th Battalion. That night he had dinner with them. New men were arriving every few minutes, and the next day, after he had been transferred to "K" Company, they continued to arrive. The nucleus of this company were officers of the original tanks, three or four of them perhaps, and the rest was made up with the newcomers.

Men continued to arrive in driblets, from the beginning of December to the first of January. When a new man joins an old regiment there is a reserve about the others which is rather chilling. They wait to see whether he is going to fit in, before they make any attempts to fit him in. In a way, this very aloofness makes for comfort on the part of the newcomer. At mess, he is left alone until he is absorbed naturally. It gives him a chance to find his level.

All this was different with the Tank Corps. With the exception of the very few officers who were "old men," we were all painfully new, so that we regarded one another without criticism and came to know each other without having to break through the wall of reserve and instinctive mistrust which is characteristically British. A happy bond of good-fellowship was formed immediately.

The first few days were spent in finding billets for the men. They were finally quartered at a hospice in the village. This was a private almshouse, in charge of a group of French nuns, where lived a number of old men and women, most of them in the last stages of consumption. The Hospice consisted of the old Abbey of Ste. Berthe, built in the twelfth century, and several outbuildings around a courtyard. In these barns lived the men, and one large room was reserved for the officers' mess. The Company

A British tank and its crew in New York

Orderly Room and Quartermaster's Stores were also kept in the Hospice, and four or five officers were quartered above the Refectory. The buildings were clean and comfortable, and the only drawback lay in the fact that one sometimes found it objectionable to have to look at these poor old creatures, dragging themselves around. They had nothing to do, it seemed, but to wait and die.

One old man was a gruesome sight. He was about ninety years old and spent his days walking about the courtyard, wearing a cigarette tin hung around his neck, into which he used to cough with such terrible effort that it seemed as if he would die every time the spasm shook him. As a matter of fact, he and many others did die before we left the village: the extreme cold was too much for them; or perhaps it was the fact that their quiet had been invaded by the "mad English." It was during this time that Talbot developed a positive genius for disappearing whenever a gray habit came into sight.

The nuns were splendid women: kind and hospitable and eager for our comfort, but they did not like to be imposed upon, however slightly. The first thing that Frenchwomen do—and these nuns were no exception—when soldiers are billeted with them, is to learn who is the officer in charge, in order that they may lose no time in bringing their complaints to him. The Mother Superior of the Hospice selected Talbot with unerring zeal. His days were made miserable, until in self-defence he thought of formulating a new calendar of "crimes" for his men, in which would be included all the terrible offences which the Mother Superior told off to him.

Did the colonel send for Captain Talbot, and did Talbot hurry off to obey the command, just so surely would the Mother Superior select that moment to bar his path.

"*Ah, mon Capitaine!*" she would exclaim, with a beaming smile. "*J'ai quelque chose à vous dire. Un soldat —*"

Talbot would break in politely, just as she had settled down for a good long chat, and explain that the colonel wished to see him. As well try to move the Rock. It was either stand and listen, or go into the presence of his superior officer with an excited nun following him with tales of the "crimes" his men had committed. Needless to say, the Mother Superior conquered. Talbot would have visions of some fairly serious offence, and would hear the tale of a soldier who had borrowed a bucket an hour ago, promising, on his honour as a soldier of the King, to return it in fifty minutes at the most.

"And it is now a full sixty minutes by the clock on the kitchen mantel, *M'sieu le Capitaine*," she would say, her colour mounting, " and your soldier has not returned my bucket. If he does not bring it back, when can we get another bucket?"

And so on, until Talbot would pacify her, promising her that the bucket would be returned. Then he would go on to the colonel, breathless and perturbed, his mind so full of buckets that there was hardly room for the business of the Tank Corps. Small wonder that the sight of a gray habit was enough to unnerve the man.

He, himself, was billeted with a French family, just around the corner from the Hospice. The head of the family had been, in the halcyon days before the war, the village butcher. There was now *Madame*, the little Marie, a sturdy boy about twelve, and the old *Grand'mère*. The husband was away, of course,—"*dans les tranchées*," explained *Madame* with copious tears.

Talbot was moved to sympathy, and made a few tactful inquiries as to where the husband was now, and how he had fared.

"*Il est maintenant à Paris*," said *Madame* with a sigh.

"In Paris! What rank has he?—a General, maybe?"

"*Ah, M'sieu s'amuse*," said *Madame*, brightening up. No, her husband was a chef at an officers' mess in Paris, she explained proudly. He had been there since the war broke out. He would soon come home, the Saints be praised. Then the captain would hear him tell his tales of life in the army!

The hero came home one day, and great was the rejoicing. Thrilling evenings the family spent around the stove while they listened to stories of great deeds. On the day when his *permission* was finished, and he set out for his hazardous post once more,

t was the lamenting. *Madame* wept. All the brave man's rela-
↲ves poured in to kiss him goodbye. The departing soldier wept,
himself. Even *Grand'mère* desisted for that day from cracking
jokes, which she was always doing in a patois that to Talbot was
unintelligible.

But they were very kind to Talbot, and very courageous
through the hard winter. When he lay ill with fever in his little
low room, where the frost whitened the plaster and icicles hung
from the ceiling, *Madame* and all the others were most solicitous
for his comfort. His appreciation and thanks were sincere.

By the middle of December the Battalion had finally settled
down and we began our training. Our first course of study was
in the mechanism of the tanks. We marched down, early one
morning, to an engine hangar that was both cold and draughty.
We did not look in the least like embryo heroes. Over our khaki
we wore ill-fitting blue garments which men on the railways,
who wear them, call "boilers."

The effect of wearing them was to cause us to slouch along,
and suddenly Talbot burst out laughing at the spectacle. Then he
remembered having heard that some of the original "Tankers"
had, during the Somme battles, been mistaken for Germans in
their blue dungarees. They had been fired on from some distance away, by their own infantry; though nothing fatal ensued.
In consequence, before the next "show" chocolate ones were
issued.

In the shadows of the engine shed, a gray armour-plated hulk
loomed up.

"There it is!" cried Gould, and started forward for a better
look at the "Willie."

Across the face of Rigden, the instructor, flashed a look of
scorn and pain. Just such a look you may have seen on the face
of a young mother when you refer to her baby as "it."

"Don't call a tank 'it,' Gould," he said with admirable patience. "A tank is either 'he' or 'she'; there is no 'it'"

"In Heaven's name, what's the difference?" asked Gould,
completely mystified. The rest of us were all ears.

"The female tank carries machine guns only," Rigden explained. "The male tank carries light field guns as well as machine guns. Don't ever make the mistake again, any of you fellows."

Having firmly fixed in our minds the fact that we were to begin on a female "Willie," the instruction proceeded rapidly. Rigden opened a little door in the side of the tank. It was about as big as the door to a large, old-fashioned brick oven built into the chimney beside the fireplace. His head disappeared and his body followed after. He was swallowed up, save for a hand that waved to us and a muffled voice which said, "Come on in, you fellows."

Gould went first. He scrambled in, was lost to sight, and then we heard his voice.

McKnutt's infectious laugh rose above the sound of our mirth. But not for long.

"Hurry up!" called Rigden. "You next, McKnutt."

McKnutt disappeared. Then to our farther astonishment his rich Irish voice could be heard upraised in picturesque malediction. What was Rigden doing to them inside the tank to provoke such profanity from them both? The rest of us scrambled to find out. We soon learned.

When you enter a tank, you go in head first, entering by the side doors. (There is an emergency exit—a hole in the roof which is used by the wise ones.) You wiggle your body in with more or less grace, and then you stand up. Then, if it is the first time, you are usually profane. For you have banged your head most unmercifully against the steel roof and you learn, once and for all, that it is impossible to stand upright in a tank. Each one of us received our baptism in this way. Seven of us, crouched in uncomfortable positions, ruefully rubbed our heads, to Rigden's intense enjoyment. Our life in a tank had begun!

We looked around the little chamber with eager curiosity. Our first thought was that seven men and an officer could never do any work in such a little place. Eight of us were, at present, jammed in here, but we were standing still. When it came to going into action and moving around inside the tank, it would be impossible,—there was no room to pass one another. So we thought.

In front are two stiff seats, one for the officer and one for the driver. Two narrow slits serve as portholes through which to look ahead. In front of the officer is a map board, and gun mounting. Behind the engine, one on each side, are the secondary gears. Down the middle of the tank is the powerful petrol engine, part of it covered with a hood, and along either side a narrow passage through which a man can slide from the officer's and driver's seat back and forth to the mechanism at the rear. There are four gun turrets, two on each side. There is also a place for a gun in the rear, but this is rarely used, for "Willies" do not often turn tail and flee!

Along the steel walls are numberless ingenious little cupboards for stores, and ammunition cases are stacked high. Every bit of space is utilized. Electric bulbs light the interior. Beside the driver are the engine levers. Behind the engine are the secondary gears, by which the machine is turned in any direction. All action inside is directed by signals, for when the tank moves the noise is such as to drown a man's voice.

All that first day and for many days after, we struggled with the intricacies of the mechanism. Sometimes, Rigden despaired of us. We might just as well go back to our regiments, unless they were so glad to be rid of us that they would refuse. On other days, he beamed with pride, even when Darwin and the Old Bird distinguished themselves by asking foolish questions. "Darwin " is, of course, not his right name. Because he came from South Africa and looked like a baboon, we called him "Baboon." So let evolution evolve the name of "Darwin" for him in these pages.

As for the Old Bird, no other name could have suited him so well. He was the craftiest old bird at successfully avoiding work we had ever known, and yet he was one of the best liked men in the company. He was one of those men who are absolutely essential to a mess because of his never-failing cheer and gaiety.

He never did a stroke of work that he could possibly "wangle" out of. A Scotchman by birth, he was about thirty-eight years old and had lived all over the world. He had a special fondness for China. Until he left "K" Company, he was never known by any other name than that of "Old Bird."

There was one man, from another Company, who gave us the greatest amusement during our Tank-mechanism Course. He was pathetically in earnest, but appeared to have no brains at all. Sometimes, while asking each other catch questions, we would put the most senseless ones to him.

Darwin would say, "Look here, how is the radiator connected with the differential?"

The poor fellow would ponder for a minute or two and then reply, "Oh! through the magneto."

He naturally failed again and again to pass his tests, and was returned to his old Corps.

Somehow we learned not to attempt to stand upright in our steel prison. Before long, McKnutt had ceased his remarks about sardines in a tin and announced, "Sure! there is plenty of room and to spare for a dozen others here." The Old Bird no longer compared the atmosphere, when we were all shut in tight, with the Black Hole of Calcutta. In a word, we had succumbed to the "Willies," and would permit no man to utter a word of criticism against them.

It is necessary here, perhaps, to explain why we always call our machines "Willies." When the tanks were first being experimented upon, they evolved two, a big and a little one Standing together they looked so ludicrous, that they were nicknamed "Big" and "Little Willie." The name stuck; and now, no one in the corps refers to his machine in any other way.

A few days before Christmas, our tank course was finished, and the Old Bird suggested a celebration. McKnutt led the cheering. Talbot had an idea.

"Let's get a box-body and go over to Amiens and do our Christmas shopping," he said.

A chorus of "Jove, that's great!" arose. Everyone made himself useful excepting the Old Bird, who made up by contributing more than anyone else to the gaiety of the occasion. The car was secured, and we all piled in, making early morning hideous with our songs.

We sped along over the snowy roads. War seemed very far away. We were extraordinarily light-hearted. After about twenty miles the cold sobered us down a little. Suddenly, the car seemed to slip from under us and we found ourselves piled up in the soft snow of the road. A rear wheel had shot off, and it went rolling along on its own. Fortunately we had been going rather slowly since we were entering a town, and no one was hurt. Borwick, the musician of the company, looked like a snow image; Darwin and the Old Bird were locked in each other's arms, and had an impromptu and friendly wrestling match in a snowdrift.

McKnutt was invoking the aid of the Saints in his endeavours to prevent the snow from trickling down his back. Talbot and Gould, who had got off lightly, supplied the laughter. The wheel was finally rescued and restored to its proper place, and we crawled along at an ignominious pace until the spires of Amiens welcomed us.

We shopped in the afternoon, buying all sorts of ridiculous things, and collecting enough stores to see us through a siege. After a hilarious dinner at the Hôtel de l'Univers (never had the Old Bird been so witty and gay), we started back about eleven o'clock, and forgetting our injured wheel, raced out of the town toward home.

A short distance down the main boulevard, the wheel again came off, and this time the damage could not be repaired. There was nothing for it but to wait until morning, and it was a disconsolate group that wandered about. All the hotels were full up. Finally, a Y.M.C.A. hut made some of us welcome. We sat about, reading and talking, until we dozed off in our chairs. The next morning we got a new wheel and ran gingerly the sixty-odd miles back, to regale the others with enviable tales of our pre-Christmas festivities.

CHAPTER 3

Later Days of Training

"Well, thank Heaven, that sweat's over," said the Old Bird the night after we finished our tank course, and had our celebration. He stretched luxuriously.

"Yes, but you're starting off again on the gun tomorrow morning," said the major, cheerfully.

The Old Bird protested.

"But I can have a few days' rest, sir, can't I?" he said sorrowfully.

The major laughed.

"No, you can't. You're down, so you'll have to go through with it."

So for three days we sat in the open, in the driving sleet, from half-past eight in the morning until half-past four in the afternoon, learning the gun. On the fourth day we finished off our course with firing on the range. Surprising as it may seem, after two or three rounds we could hit the very smallest object at a distance of four or five hundred yards.

"How many more courses must we go through?" asked the Old Bird of Rigden, as they strolled back one evening from the range. The Old Bird was always interested in how much—or, rather, how little—work he had before him.

"There's the machine gun; the signalling course,—you'll have to work hard on that, but I know you don't object,—and also revolver practice. Aren't you thrilled?"

"No, I'm not," grumbled the Old Bird. " Life isn't worth living with all this work to do. I wish we could get into action."

"So do I," said Talbot, joining them. "But while we're waiting, wouldn't you rather be back here with good warm billets and a comfortable bed and plenty to eat, instead of sitting in a wet trench with the Infantry?" He remembered an old man in his regiment who had been with the Salvation Army at home. He would stump along on his flat feet, trudging miles with his pack on his back, and Talbot had never heard him complain. He was bad at drill. He could never get the orders or formations through his head. Talbot had often lost patience with him, but the old fellow was always cheerful.

One morning, in front of Bapaume, after a night of terrible cold, the old man could not move. Talbot tried to cheer him up and to help him, but he said feebly: "I think I'm done for—I don't believe I shall ever get warm. But never mind, sir." And in a few minutes he died, as uncomplainingly as he had lived.

"You're right, of course, Talbot," the Old Bird said. "We're very well off here. But, I say, how I should like to be down in Boulogne for a few days!" And until they reached the mess, the Old Bird dilated on the charm of Boulogne and all the luxuries he would indulge in the next time he visited the city.

The rest of that week found us each day parading at eight o'clock in the courtyard of the Hospice, and after instruction the various parties marched off to their several duties. Some of us went to the tankdrome; some of us to the hills overlooking historic Agincourt, and others to the barn by the railroad where we practised with the guns. Another party accompanied Borwick to a secluded spot where he drilled them in machine-gun practice. Borwick was as skilful with a machine gun as with a piano. This was the highest praise one could give him.

That night at mess, Gould said suddenly:—"Tomorrow's a half day, isn't it?"

"Of course. Wake up, you idiot," said Talbot. "We're playing 'J' Company at soccer, and on Sunday we're playing 'L' at rugger. Two strenuous days before us. Are you feeling fit?"

Gould was feeling most awfully fit. In fact, he assured the mess that he, alone, was a match for "J" Company.

Our soccer team was made up almost entirely of men who had been professional players. We had great pride in them, so that on the following afternoon, an eager crowd streamed out of the village to our football field, which we had selected with great care. It was as flat as a cricket pitch. A year ago it had been ploughed as part of the French farmland, and now here were the English playing football!

Before the game began there was a good deal of cheerful chaffing on the respective merits of the "J" and "K" Company teams. And when the play was in progress and savage yells rent the air, the French villagers looked on in wonder and pity. They had always believed the English to be mad. Now they were convinced of it.

From the outset, however, "J" Company was hopelessly outclassed, and wishing to be generous to a failing foe, we ceased our wild cheering. "J" Company, on the other hand, wishing to exhort their team to greater efforts, made up for our moderation, with the result that our allies were firmly convinced that "J" Company had won the game! If not, why should they dance up and down and wave their hats and shriek? And even the score, five to one in favour of "K" Company, failed to convince them entirely. But "K" went home to an hilarious tea, with a sense of work well done.

And what of the rugger game the next day? Let us draw a veil over it. Suffice it to say that the French congratulated "K" Company over the outcome of that, although the score was twelve to three in favour of "J"!

We awoke on Monday morning with a delightful feeling that something pleasant was going to happen, for all the world the same sensation we used to experience on waking on our birthday and suddenly remembering that gifts were sure to appear and that there would be something rather special for tea! By the time full consciousness returned, we remembered that this was the day when, for the first time, the tank was to be set in motion.

Even the Old Bird was eager.

We hurry off to the tankdrome. One after another we slide in through the little door and are swallowed up. The door is bolted behind the last to enter. Officer and driver slip into their respective seats. The steel shutters of the portholes click as they are opened. The gunners take their positions. The driver opens the throttle a little and tickles the carburettor, and the engine is started up. The driver races the engine a moment, to warm her up. The officer reaches out a hand and signals for first speed On each gear; the driver throws his lever into first; he opens the throttle: the tank—our "Willie"—moves!

Supposing you were locked in a steel box, with neither portholes to look through nor air-holes to breathe from. Supposing you felt the steel box begin to move, and, of course, were unable to see where you were going. Can you imagine the sensation? Then you can guess the feelings of the men in a tank, excepting the officer and driver, who can see ahead through their portholes,—when the monster gets under way. There are times, of course, with the bullets flying thick and fast, when all portholes, for officer, driver, and gunners, must be closed. Then we plunge ahead, taking an occasional glimpse through the special pin-point holes.

Thirty tons of steel rolls along with its human freight. Suddenly, the driver rings a bell. He presses another button, and signals the driver of the right-hand track into "neutral." This disconnects the track from the engine. The tank swings around to the right. The right-hand driver gets the signal "First speed," and we are off again, at a right angle to our former direction.

Now we are headed for a gentle slope across the field, and as we approach it, the tank digs her nose into the base of the hill. She crawls up. The men in the rear tip back and enjoy it hugely. If the hill is steep enough they may even find themselves lying flat on their backs or standing on their heads! But no such luck. Presently they are standing as nearly upright as it is ever possible to stand, and the tank is balancing on the top of the slope. The driver is not expert as yet, and we go over with an awful jolt and tumble forward. This is rare fun!

But the instructor is not pleased. We must try it all over again. So back again to attack the hill a second time. The top is reached once more and we balance there. The driver throws out his clutch, we slip over very gently, and carefully he lets the clutch in again and down we go. The "Willie" flounders around for the fraction of a second. Then, nothing daunted, she starts off once more. We have visions of her sweeping all before her someday far behind the German lines.

Three or four weeks of this sort of thing, and we are hardened to it.

Our reward came at last, however. After mess one morning, when the conversation had consisted mainly of the question, "When are we going into a show?" with no answer to the question, we were called into the major's room, where he told us, in strictest secrecy, that in about three weeks a big attack was to come off. We should go in at last!

For the next two or three weeks we studied maps and aeroplane photographs, marking out our routes, starting-points, rear ammunition-dumps, forward dumps, and lines of supply. At last, then, our goal loomed up and these months of training, for the most part interesting, but at times terribly boring, would bear fruit. Two direct results were noticeable now on looking back to the time when we joined. First, each man in the battalion knew how to run a tank, how to effect slight repairs, how to work the guns, and how to obtain the best results from the machine.

Second, and very important, was the fact that the men and officers had got together. The crews and officers of each section knew and trusted each other. The strangeness of feeling that was apparent in the first days had now entirely disappeared, and that cohesion of units which is so essential in warfare had been accomplished. Each of us knew the other's faults and the mistakes he was prone to make. More important still, we knew our own faults and weaknesses and had the courage to carry on and overcome them.

A few nights before we moved up the line, we gave a grand

concert. Berwick and the Old Bird planned it. On an occasion of this sort, the Old Bird never grumbled at the amount of work he was obliged to do. Some weeks before we had bought a piano from one of the inhabitants of the village, and the piano was naturally the *pièce de résistance* of the concert. The Old Bird went around for days at a time, humming scraps of music with unintelligible words which it afterwards developed at the concert were awfully good songs of his own composing. The battalion tailor was called in to make up rough Pierrot costumes. The Old Bird drilled us until we begged for mercy, while Berwick strummed untiringly at the piano. At last the great night arrived.

A stage had been built at one end of a hangar, and curtains hung up.

The whole of the Staff and H.Q. had been invited, and the *maire*, the *curé*, the *médecin* of the village, and their families were also to attend.

Promptly at eight o'clock, the concert began, with Berwick at the piano. Everything went off without a hitch. Although "K" Company provided most of the talent, the battalion shared the honours of the entertainment. Each song had a chorus, and so appreciative was our audience that the choruses were repeated again and again. The one "lady" of the *troupe* looked charming, and "she" arranged for "her" voice to be entirely in keeping with "her" dress and paint. The French spectators enjoyed it hugely. They were a great encouragement, for they laughed at everything uproariously, though it could not have been due to their understanding of the jokes.

At ten o'clock we finished off with "God Save the King," and went back to our billets feeling that our stay in the village had been splendidly rounded off.

CHAPTER 4

Moving up the Line

Two or three days before we were due to leave, we had received orders to pack our surplus kit, and have it at the Quartermaster's Stores at a certain time. We drew a long breath. This meant that the actual date, which up to the present had been somewhat indefinite, was close at hand. We were given orders to draw our tanks and the whole Company was marched over to work sheds about two miles away at E——, where tanks and stores were issued.

The variety and number of little things which it is necessary to draw when fitting out a tank for action is inconceivable. Tools, small spares, Pyrenes, electric lamps, clocks, binoculars, telescopes, petrol and oil funnels, oil squirts, grease guns, machine guns, headlights, tail lamps, steel hawsers, crowbars, shovels, picks, inspection lamps, and last, but not least, ammunition. The field-gun ammunition has to be taken out of its boxes and placed in the shell racks inside the tank.

The S.A.A. (small arms ammunition) must be removed from its boxes and stacked away. At the same time every single round, before being put into the drum, must be gauged. All this has to be done in the last two or three days, and everything must be checked and countersigned. There is always a great deal of fun for tank commanders in drawing their stores. It is a temptation, when in the midst of all these thousands of articles, to seize the opportunity, when no one is looking, to pocket a few extra spares and dainty little tools, not, of course, for one's own personal benefit, but simply because such things are always being lost or stolen, and it is exasperating, to say the least, to find one's self, at a critical moment, without some article which it is impossible to duplicate at the time.

During these last few days it was a continual march for the men from B—— to E——.

Very often they were called back when their day's work was over to draw some new article or make some alteration which had been forgotten at the time they were in the workshops.

At last, however,—on the third day following the grand concert,—the kits were packed, loaded on to the lorries, and sent off to E——.

The troops said "Goodbye" to the village which had been such a happy home and school during that winter of 1916, and the officers made their fond *adieus* to the mothers and daughters of the houses in which they had been billeted.

The companies formed up and marched along to the workshops. Everyone was in high spirits, and there was a friendly race to see which Company of the Battalion could load up their tanks in the shortest time on to the specially constructed steel trucks.

A few days before all these activities commenced, Talbot and another tank commander had gone on to the tanks' ultimate destination, A——, a village which had been evacuated a few days before by the Germans on their now famous retirement to the Hindenburg Line. It was a most extraordinary sight to ride along the road from Albert to Bapaume, which during the summer and winter of the preceding year had witnessed such heavy fighting. The whole country on each side of the road was a desolate *vista* of shell-holes as far as the eye could see.

Where villages had been, there was now no trace left of any sort of habitation. One might think that, however heavy a bombardment, some trace would be left of the village which had suffered. There was literally nothing left of the village through which had run the road they were now travelling. Over this scarred stretch of country were dotted camps and groups of huts, with duck-boards crossing the old shell-holes, some of which were still full of water.

On approaching B—— they saw traces everywhere of the methodical and organized methods by which the Germans had retired. The first sign was a huge shell-crater in the middle of the road, about forty feet deep, which the Boche had arranged to prevent armoured cars from following him up. If they did succeed, the transports would be delayed in reaching them, at all events. These holes were rather a nuisance, for the road itself was a mass of lesser shell-craters and the soft ground on each side was impassable. The road was crowded with engineers and labour battalions, filling in the shell-holes, and laying railways into the outskirts of A——.

In A—— the old German notices were still standing as they had been left. Strung across the road on a wire was a notice which read: "*Fuhrweg nach Behagnies.*" Every house in the town had been pulled down. The wily Boche had not even blown them up. Instead he had saved explosives by attaching steel hawsers to the houses and by means of tractors had pulled them down, so that the roof and sides fell in on the foundation. Every pump handle in the village had been broken off short, and not a single piece of furniture was left behind. Later, we found the furniture from this and other villages in the Hindenburg Line.

Saddest of all, however, was the destruction of the beautiful poplar trees which once bordered the long French roads built by Napoleon. These had been sawn off at their base and allowed to fall on the side of the road, not across it, as one might suppose. If they had been allowed to fall across the road, the Boche, himself, would have been hindered in his last preparations for his retreat.

Everything was done with military ends in view. The villages were left in such a condition as to make them uninhabitable, the more to add to our discomfort and to make our hardships severer. The trees were cut down only on those parts of the road which were screened from observation from his balloons and present trenches. In some places where the road dipped into a valley the trees had been left untouched.

At the place where our tanks were scheduled to arrive, and which had lately been a railhead of the Boche, all the metals had been torn up, and in order to destroy the station itself, he had smashed the cast-iron pillars which supported the roof, and in consequence the whole building had fallen in. But nothing daunted, the British engineers were even now working at top speed laying down new lines.

Some of the metals, which a few short weeks before had been lying in countless stacks down on the quays at the Bases, now unrolled themselves at the rate of about two and a quarter miles a day. One interesting feature of this rapid track-laying was that when the tank train left E——— , on its two and a half days' journey down to the railhead at A———, the track on which the train was to run was not completed into A———. But, nevertheless, the track arrived ahead of the train, which was the main point!

As they rode into the ruined village of A——— Talbot and his companion came across still further evidence of the steps which the German will take to inconvenience his enemy. In order to battle against the hordes of rats which are so prevalent in the old parts of the line in France, the Boche breeds cats in enormous numbers. Yet, in order to carry out to the limit his idea that nothing of value should fall into our hands, he had killed every cat in the village. In every house three or four of these poor little creatures lay around with their heads chopped off. Tabby cats, black cats, white cats, and little kittens, all dead. Farther on, over a well at the corner of the main square was posted a sign which read: "This well is poisoned. Do not touch. By order. R.E."

Here and there a house had been left intact, with its furniture untouched. It was not until later that it struck us as peculiar that these houses had been spared from the general destruction. Two or three days later, however, after we had moved in, and head-quarters had been established, we discovered that under many of these houses, and at certain crossroads which had not been blown up in the usual manner, the Boche had left mines, timed to go off at any time up to twenty-eight days.

One could never be sure that the ground underneath one's feet would not blow up at any moment. These mines were small boxes of high explosive, inside of which was a little metal tube with trigger and detonator attached. Inside the tube was a powerful acid, which, when it had eaten its way through, set free the trigger and exploded the charge. The length of time it took for the mine to explode was gauged by the strength or weakness of the acid in the tube.

We were also impressed with the mechanical genius of the German. The Boche had made a veritable mechanical toy out of nearly every house in the village which he had spared. Delightful little surprises had been prepared for us everywhere. Kick a harmless piece of wood, and in a few seconds a bomb exploded. Pick up a bit of string from the floor and another bomb went off. Soon we learned to be wary of the most innocent objects. Before touching anything we made elaborate preparations for our safety.

One of the men was greatly annoyed by a wire which hung over his head when he was asleep, but he did not wish to remove it. He had decided that it was connected with some devilish device which would do him no good. Finally, one morning, he could endure this sword of Damocles no longer. With two boon companions, he carefully attached a string about fifteen yards long to the wire. They tiptoed gently out of the house to a discreet distance, and with a yell of triumph, the hero pulled the string,—and nothing happened!

But there was another side to all this. McKnutt some time afterwards came in with an interesting story. Some Sappers, he said, had been digging under a house in the village, presumably for the mysterious reasons that always drive the Engineers to dig in unlikely places. One of them pushed his shovel into what had been the cellar of the house, but as the roof had fallen in on the entrance, they did not know of its existence.

When they finally forced their way in, they found two German officers and two Frenchwomen in a terribly emaciated

A TANK MOVING TO THE ATTACK
DOWN WHAT WAS ONCE A MAIN STREET

condition. One of the Boches and one of the women lay dead, locked in each other's arms. The other two still breathed, but when they were brought up into the open they expired within a few hours without either of them giving an explanation. The only reason we could find for their terrible plight was that the women had been forced down there by the officers to undergo a last farewell, while the Germans were destroying the village, and that the house had fallen in on top of them.

Later, probably no one knew where they had disappeared, and they were unable to get out of the ruins or to make themselves heard. The village of A—— gained a romantic reputation after that, and it was curious to realize that we had been living there for days while this silent tragedy was being enacted.

In addition to the destruction in the towns, the beautiful orchards which are so numerous in France were ruined. Apple, pear, and plum trees lay uprooted on the ground, and here again the military mind of the German had been at work. He did not wish the fruit that the trees would bear in future to fall into our hands.

But although the village was a pretty poor place in which to stay, the near presence of a B.E.F. Canteen was a comfort. It is always amazing to visit one of these places. Within perhaps four or five miles of the firing line we have stores selling everything from a silver cigarette case to a pair of boots, and everything, too, at nearly cost price. The canteen provides almost every variety of smoking materials, and eatables, and their only disadvantage is that they make packages from home seem so useless.

As the tobaccos come straight out of bond, it is far cheaper to buy them at the canteen, than to have them forwarded from home. These canteens are managed by the army, and are dotted all over the country inhabited by the British troops. Since they have sprung into existence life at the front has been far more comfortable and satisfactory in France, and people at home are discovering that money is the best thing to send out to their men.

Finally, one cold, sunny morning, about half-past five, the

tank train steamed slowly into A——, and drew up on a siding. It was not possible to begin the work of unloading the tanks until night fell. So the tired crews turned into the roofless houses which had been prepared for them, and slept until dusk. When darkness fell, as if by magic, the town sprang to activity.

CHAPTER 5

Preparations for the Show

That night the engines were started up, and one by one the tanks crawled off the train. Although the day had begun with brilliant sunshine, at dusk the snow had begun to fall, and by the time the tanks came off, the snow was a foot thick on the ground. The tanks moved down to the temporary tankdrome which had been decided upon near the railway, and the sponson trucks were towed there. The night was spent in fitting on the sponsons to the sides of the machines. It was bitterly cold. The sleet drove in upon us all night, stinging our hands and faces. Everything seemed to go wrong. We had the utmost difficulty in making the bolt-holes fit, and as each sponson weighs about three tons they were not easy to move and adjust. We drove ahead with the work, knowing that it must be done while the darkness lasted.

Finally, about two hours before dawn broke, the last bolt was fastened, and the tanks were ready to move. The night was blacker than ever as they lumbered out of the tankdrome, and were led across the snow to a halfway house about four miles from the railhead, and an equal distance from the front-line trenches. We had not quite reached our destination when the darkness began to lift in the east, and with feverish energy we pushed ahead, through the driving snow.

Late that afternoon, Talbot was again sent ahead with five or six troopers and orderlies to a village in the front line. It was necessary for us to spend three or four days there before the attack commenced, in order to study out the vulnerable points in the German line. We were to decide also the best routes for the tanks to take in coming up to the line, and those to be taken later in crossing No Man's Land when the "show" was on.

We rode along across fields denuded of all their trees. The country here was utterly unlike that to which we had been accustomed in "peace-time trench warfare." This last expression sounds like an anomaly, but actually it means the life which is led in trenches where one may go along for two or three months without attacking. In comparison with our existence when we are making an offensive, the former seems like life in peace times. Hence, the expression. But from this it must not be supposed that "peace-time trench warfare" is all beer and skittles. Quite the contrary.

As a matter of fact, during four or five days in the trenches there may be as many casualties as during an attack, but taking it on an average, naturally the losses and dangers are greater when troops go over the top. Curiously enough, too, after one has been in an attack the front-line trench seems a haven of refuge. Gould, who was wounded in the leg during a battle on the Somme, crawled into a shell-hole. It was a blessed relief to be lying there, even though the bullets were whistling overhead. At first he felt no pain, and he wished, vaguely, that he had brought a magazine along to read!

All through the burning summer day he stayed there, waiting for the night. As soon as it was dark he wriggled back to our trenches, tumbled over the parapet of the front-line trench, and narrowly escaped falling on the point of a bayonet. But he never forgets the feeling of perfect safety and peace at being back, even in an exposed trench, with friends.

The fields across which we rode had been ploughed the preceding autumn by the French civilians. Later, when the snow had disappeared, we could see where the ground had been torn up by the horses of a German riding-school of ten days before. On some of the roads the ruts and heavy marks of the retreating German transports could still be seen. It was a new and exciting experience to ride along a road which only two or three days before had been traversed by the Germans in a retreat, even though they called it a "retirement." The thought was very pleasant to men who, for the last two years, had been sitting in front of the Boche month after month, and who, even in an attack, had been unable to find traces of foot, hoof, or wheel mark because of the all-effacing shell-fire.

Here and there were places where the Boche had had his watering-troughs, and also the traces of scattered huts and tents on the ground where the grass, of a yellowish green, still showed. The front line of defence here was really no front line at all, but was merely held as in open warfare by outposts, sentry groups, and patrols.

At night it was the easiest thing in the world to lose one's self close up to the line and wander into the German trenches. In fact, over the whole of this country, where every landmark had been destroyed and where owing to the weather the roads were little different from the soil on each side, a man could lose himself and find no person or any sign to give him his direction. The usual guide which one might derive from the Verey lights going up between the lines was here non-existent, as both sides kept extremely quiet. Even the guns were comparatively noiseless in these days, and were a man to find himself at night alone upon this ground, which lay between two and three miles behind our own lines, the only thing he could do would be to lie down and wait for the dawn to show him the direction.

As we rode toward O—— our only guide was a few white houses two or three miles away on the edge of the village. The German had not evacuated O—— of his own free will, but a certain "Fighting Division" had taken the village two days before and driven the German out, when he retired three or four hundred yards farther to his rear Hindenburg Line. The probable reason why he hung on to this village, which was really in front of his line of advance, was because at the time he decided to retire on the Somme, the Hindenburg Line was incomplete. In fact, the Boche could still be seen working on his wire and trenches.

We arrived in O—— at nightfall. Some batteries were behind the village, and the Germans were giving the village and the guns a rather nasty time. Unhappily for us, the Boche artillery were dropping five-nine's on the road which led into the village, and as they seemed unlikely to desist, we decided to make a dash for it. The horses were a bit nervous, but behaving very well under the trying circumstances. (With us were some limbers bringing up ammunition.) Shells were exploding all around us. It would never do to stand still.

The dash up that hundred yards of road was an unpleasant experience. As we made the rush, the gunners tearing along "hell for leather" and the others galloping ahead on their plunging horses, we heard the dull whistle and the nearer roar of two shells approaching. Instinctively we leaned forward. We held our breath. When a shell drops near, there is always the feeling that it is going to fall on one's head. We flattened ourselves out and urged our horses to greater speed. The shells exploded about thirty yards behind us, killing two gunners and their mules, while the rest of us scrambled into the village and under cover.

In the darkness, we found what had once been the shop of the village blacksmith, and in the forge we tied up our horses. It was bitterly cold. It was either make a fire and trust to luck that it would not be observed, or freeze.

We decided on the fire, and in its grateful warmth we lay down to snatch the first hours of sleep we had had in nearly three days. But the German gunners were most inconsiderate, and a short time afterward they dropped a small barrage down the road. The front of our forge was open, and we were obliged to flatten ourselves on the ground to prevent the flying splinters from hitting us. When this diversion was over, we stirred up our fire, and made some tea, just in time to offer some to a gunner sergeant who came riding up. He hitched his horse to one of the posts, and sat down with us by the fire. The shell-fire had quieted down, and we dozed off, glad of the interlude. Suddenly a shell burst close beside us. The poor beast, waiting patiently for

48

his rider, was hit in the neck by the shrapnel, but hardly a sound escaped him.

In war, especially, one cannot help admiring the stoicism of horses, as compared with other animals. One sees examples of it on all sides. Tread, for instance, on a dog's foot, and he runs away, squealing. A horse is struck by a large lump of shrapnel just under its withers, and the poor brute trembles, but makes no sound. Almost the only time that horses scream—and the sound is horrible—is when they are dying. Then they shriek from sheer pain and fear. Strange as it may seem, one is often more affected by seeing horses struck than when men are killed. Somehow they seem so particularly helpless.

It was during these days at O—— that Talbot discovered Johnson. Johnson was one of his orderlies. Although it did not lie in the path of his duty, he took the greatest delight in doing all sorts of little odd jobs for Talbot. So unobtrusive he was about it all, that for some time Talbot hardly noticed that someone was trying to make him comfortable. When he did, by mutual agreement Johnson became his servant and faithful follower through everything. The man was perfectly casual and apparently unaffected by the heaviest shell-fire.

It is absurd to say that a man "doesn't mind shell-fire." Everyone dislikes it, and gets nervous under it. The man who "doesn't mind it" is the man who fights his nervousness and gets such control of himself that he is able to appear as if he were unaffected. Between "not minding it" and "appearing not to mind it" lie hard-won moral battles, increased strength of character, and victory over fear. Johnson had accomplished this. He preserved an attitude of careless calm, and could walk down a road with shells bursting all around him with a sublime indifference that was inspiring. Between him and his officer sprang up an extraordinary and lasting affection.

The wretched night in the forge at last came to an end, and the next morning we looked around for more comfortable billets. We selected the cellar of a house in fairly good condition and prepared to move in, when we discovered that we were not the first to whom it had appealed. Two dead Germans still occupied the premises, and when we had disposed of the bodies, we took up our residence. Here we stayed, going out each day to find the best points from which to view No Man's Land, which lay in front of the village. With the aid of maps, we planned the best routes for the tanks to take when the battle should have begun. Not a detail was neglected.

Then something happened to break the monotony of life. Just back of the village one of our batteries was concealed in such a fashion that it was impossible to find it from an aeroplane. Yet every day, regularly, the battery was shelled. Every night under cover of the darkness, the position was changed, and the battery concealed as cleverly as before, but to no avail. The only solution was that some one behind our lines was in communication with the Germans, every day. Secrecy was increased. Guards were doubled to see that no one slipped through the lines. Signals were watched. The whole affair was baffling, and yet we could find no clue.

Just in front of the wood where the battery was concealed, stood an old farmhouse where a genial Frenchwoman lived and dispensed good cheer to us. She had none of the men of her own family nor any farmhands to help her, but kept up the farmwork all alone. Every day, usually in the middle of the morning, she went out to the fields behind her house and ploughed, with an old white horse drawing the plough.

For some reason she never ploughed more than one or two furrows at a time, and when this was done, she drove the white horse back to the barn. One day, an officer noticed that a German plane hovered over the field while the woman was ploughing, and that when she went back to the house, the plane shot away. The next day the same thing happened. Later in the day, the battery received its daily reminder from the Boche gunners, as unerringly accurate as ever.

Here was a clue. The solution of the problem followed. The woman knew the position of the battery, and every day when she went out to plough, she drove the white horse up and down,

A TANK GOING OVER A TRENCH ON ITS WAY INTO ACTION

making a furrow directly in front of the battery. When the men in the German plane saw the white horse, they flew overhead, took a photograph of the newly turned furrow, and turned the photograph over to their gunners. The rest was easy.

The next day we missed three events which had become part of our daily life. The German plane no longer hovered in the air. Our battery, for the first time in weeks, spent a peaceful day. And in the field behind her house, a woman with an old white horse no longer made the earth ready for the sowing.

For three days now we had received no rations, and were obliged to subsist on the food which the Boche had left behind him when he fled. Finally, when all our plans were complete, we were notified that the point of attack had been shifted to N——, a village about four miles away. This practical joke we thought in extremely bad taste, but there was nothing for it but to pack up and move as quickly as possible. We learned that our troops at N—— had tried twice to break through the German lines by bombing. A third attempt was to be made, and the tanks were depended upon to open the way. Hence the change in our plans.

Early the next morning we left O——, and dashed along a road which lay parallel with our line, and was under direct observation from the German trenches. Owing to the fact, probably, that he was not properly settled in his new line, the Boche did not bother us much, excepting at one place, where we were obliged to make a run for it. We arrived at N—— just after the tanks had been brought up. They were hurriedly concealed close up to houses, in cuttings, and under trees.

The show was scheduled to come off the next morning at 4.30. That night we gathered at Brigade Headquarters and made the final plans. Each tank had its objective allotted to it, and marked out on the tank commander's course. Each tank was to go just so far and no farther. Talbot and Darwin were detailed to go forward as far as possible on foot when the battle was in progress, and send back messages as to how the show was progressing. Talbot also was given the task of going out that night to make the marks in No Man's Land which would guide the tanks in the morning.

At eleven o'clock, in the bright moonlight, Talbot, with Johnson and a couple of orderlies, started out. They climbed over the front line, which was at present a railway embankment, crawled into No Man's Land, and set to work. Immediately the Boche snipers spotted them and bullets began to whistle over their heads. Luckily, no one was hit, but a couple of "whizz bangs" dropped uncomfortably close. The men dropped for cover. Only Johnson stood still, his figure black against the white snow gleaming in the moonlight.

The shells continued to fall about them as they wriggled back when the work was done.

As they reached N—— the tanks were being led up toward the line, so that later, under cover of the darkness, they might be taken farther forward to their starting-points.

CHAPTER 6

The First Battle

At dawn the next morning, the tanks were already lined up, sullen and menacing in the cold half-light. The men shivered in the biting air. One by one the crews entered the machines, and one by one the little steel doors closed behind them. The engines throbbed, and they moved off sluggishly.

Darwin and Talbot, with their orderlies, waited impatiently. The moments just before an attack are always the hardest. A few batteries were keeping up a desultory fire. They glanced at their watches.

"Only a minute to go," said Darwin. "I bet the show's put off or something. Isn't this snow damnably cold, though!"

Suddenly a sixty-pounder in our rear crashed out. Then from all sides a deafening roar burst forth and the barrage began. As we became accustomed to the intensity and ear-splittingness of the sound, the bark of the eighteen-pounders could be faintly distinguished above the dull roar of the eight-inches. The sky-line was lit up with thousands of flashes, large and small, each one showing, for a second, trenches or trees or houses, and during this tornado we knew that the "Willies" must have started forward on their errand.

As the barrage lifted and the noise died down a little, the first streaks of light began to show in the sky, although we could distinguish nothing. No sign of the infantry or of the tanks could be seen. But the ominous sound of machine guns and heavy rifle-fire told us that the Boche was prepared.

A TANK HALF-WAY OVER THE TOP AND AWAITING THE ORDER TO ADVANCE IN THE BATTLE OF MINEN ROAD

We could stand this inactivity no longer. We trudged forward through the snow, taking the broad bands left by the tracks of the busses as our guide, the officers leading the way and the orderlies behind in single file.

"The blighter's starting, himself, now," said Talbot, as a four-two landed a hundred yards away, and pieces of earth came showering down on our heads. Then another and another fell, each closer than the one before, and instinctively we quickened our steps, for it is difficult to walk slowly through shell-fire.

The embankment loomed before us, and big splotches of black and yellow leaped from its surface. The deafening crashes gave us that peculiar feeling in the stomach which danger alone can produce. We scrambled up the crumbling, slaggy sides, and found when we reached the top that the sound of the machine guns had died away, excepting on the extreme left in front of B——, where the ordinary tap of ones and twos had developed into a sharp crackle of tens and twenties. By listening carefully one could feel, rather than hear, the more intermittent bursts from the rifles.

"There's one, sir," shouted one of the orderlies.

"Where?"

"Half-right and about five hundred yards ahead."

By dint of straining, we discovered a little animal—or so it looked—crawling forward on the far side of the Hindenburg Line. Already it was doing a left incline in accordance with its instructions, so as to enfilade a communication trench which ran back to N——. The German observer had spotted her. Here and there, on each side of her, a column of dirt and snow rose into the air. But the little animal seemed to bear a charmed life. No harm came to her, and she went calmly on her way, for all the world like a giant tortoise at which one vainly throws clods of earth.

As it grows lighter, we can now see others in the distance. One is not moving—is it out of action? The only motion on the whole landscape is that of the bursting shells, and the tanks. Over the white snow in front of the German wire, are dotted little black lumps. Some crawl, some move a leg or an arm, and some lie quite still. One who has never seen a modern battle doubtless forms a picture of masses of troops moving forward in splendid formation, with cheering voices and gleaming bayonets. This is quite erroneous. To an observer in a post or in a balloon, no concerted action is visible at all. Here and there a line or two of men dash forward and disappear. A single man or a small group of men wriggle across the ground. That is all.

"Well, they haven't got it in the neck as I supposed," said Darwin. "Remarkably few lying about. Let's push on."

"All right," Talbot assented. "If you like." We crawled over the top of the embankment and continued down the side. About two hundred yards to the left, we saw one of the tanks, with her nose in the air. A little group of three or four men were digging around her, frantically. We rushed over to them, and found that the Old Bird's 'bus had failed to get over a large pit which lay in the middle of No Man's Land, and was stuck with her tail in the bottom of the ditch.

Here occurred one of those extraordinary instances of luck which one notices everywhere in a modern battle. The tank had been there about ten minutes when the German gunners had bracketed on her, and were dropping five-nines, all of them within a radius of seventy yards of the tank, and yet no one was hurt. Finally, by dint of strenuous digging, she started up and pulled herself wearily out of the pit.

Suddenly, Darwin shouted:—

"Look here, you fellows! What are these Boches doing?"

Looking up, we saw about forty or fifty Germans stumbling over their own wire, and running toward us as hard as they could go. For a moment we thought it was the preliminary step of a counter-attack, but suddenly we discovered that they carried no arms and were attempting to run with their hands above their heads. At the same time something occurred which is always one of the saddest sights in war. One hears a great deal about the "horrors of war" and the "horrors" of seeing men killed on either side of one, but at the time there is very little "horror" to it. One simply doesn't have time to pay any attention to it all. But the sad part was that the German machine gunners, seeing their men surrendering, opened a furious fire on them. There they were, caught from behind, and many of them dropped from the bullets of their own comrades.

Twenty or thirty of them came straight on, rushed up to the pit where the tank had come to grief, and tumbled down into this refuge. Evidently, they knew of the British passion for souvenirs, for when our men surrounded them, the Germans plucked wildly at their own shoulder straps as if to entreat their captors to take the shoulder straps instead of anything else!

We gave two or three of the wounded Germans some cigarettes and a drink of water. They were then told to find their quickest way to the rear. Like other German prisoners we had seen, they went willingly enough. German discipline obtains even after a man has been made a prisoner. He obeys his captors with the same docility with which he had previously obeyed his own officers. Left to themselves, and started on the right road, the prisoner will plod along, their N.C.O.'s saluting the English officers, and inquiring the way to the concentration camp. When they find it, they usually appear well pleased.

The Old Bird's tank moved on.

"I suppose everything's going all right," said Talbot. "Suppose we move on and see if we can get some information."

"Yes, or some souvenirs," Darwin replied with a laugh.

We pushed on slowly. Three tanks which had completed their job were coming back and passed us. A little later we met some fellows who were slightly wounded and asked them how the battle was going. Every story was different. The wounded are rarely able to give a correct version of any engagement, and we saw that no accurate information was to be gleaned from these men.

We had been out now for an hour and a half and still had no news to send back to Headquarters. We knew how hard it was for the officers behind the lines, who had planned the whole show, to sit hour after hour waiting for news of their troops. The minutes are like hours.

"My God, Darwin, look!" Talbot cried. "Something's happened to her. She's on fire!"

In the distance we saw one of our tanks stuck in the German wire, which at that point was about a hundred yards thick. Smoke was belching from every porthole. A shell had registered a direct hit, exploding the petrol, and the tank was on fire. We dashed forward toward her.

A German machine gun rattled viciously. They had seen us. An instant later, the bullets were spattering around us, and we dropped flat. One man slumped heavily and lay quite still. By inches we crawled forward, nearer and nearer to the blazing monster. Another machine gun snarled at us, and we slid into a shell-hole for protection. Then, after a moment's breathing space, we popped out and tried to rush again. Another man stopped a bullet.

It was suicide to go farther. Into another shell-hole we fell, and thought things over. We decided to send a message, giving roughly the news that the Hindenburg Line and N—— had been taken. An orderly was given a message. He crawled out of the shell-hole, ran a few steps, dropped flat, wriggled along across the snow, sprang to his feet, ran another few steps, and so on until we lost sight of him.

A moment or two later we started across the snow in a direction parallel with the lines. Behind an embankment we came across a little group of Australians at an impromptu dressing-station. Some of them were wounded and the others were binding up their wounds. We watched them for a while and started on again. We had gone about fifty yards when a shell screeched overhead. We turned and saw it land in the middle of the group we had just left. Another shell burst close to us and huge clods of earth struck us in the face and in the stomach, knocking us flat and blinding us for the moment.

A splinter struck Talbot on his tin hat, grazing his skin. Behind us one of the orderlies screamed and we rushed back to him. He had been hit below the knee and his leg was nearly severed. We tied him up and managed to get him back to the Australian aid-post. Two of the original four stretcher-bearers had been blown up a few minutes before. But the remaining two were carrying on with their work as though nothing had happened. Here he was bandaged and started on his way for the dressing-station.

Far across the snow, we saw three more tanks plodding back toward the rear. Little by little, we gained ground until we reached a more sheltered area where we could make greater speed. We were feverishly anxious to know the fate of the crew of the burning tank. "Whose tank was it?" was on every tongue. We met other wounded men being helped back; those with leg wounds were being supported by others less seriously wounded. They could tell us nothing. They had been with the infantry and only knew that two tanks were right on the other side of the village.

A moment or two later, Talbot started running toward two men, one of whom was supporting the other. The wounded man proved to be the sergeant of the tank we had seen on fire. We hurried up to him. He was hurt in the leg. So, instead of firing questions at him, we kept quiet and accompanied him back to the dressing-station.

Later we heard the tragic news that it was Gould's tank that had burned up. None of us talked much about it. It did not seem real.

They had got stuck in the German wire. A crump had hit them and fired the petrol tank. That was the end. Two men, the sergeant and another, escaped from the tank. The others perished with it. We tried to comfort each other by repeated assurances that they must all have lost consciousness quickly from the fumes of the petrol before they suffered from fire. But it was small consolation. Everyone had liked Gould and everyone would miss him.

We waited at Brigade Headquarters for the others to return. A tank commander from another company was brought in, badly wounded and looking ghastly, but joking with everyone, as they carried him along on a stretcher. His tank had been knocked out and they had saved their guns and gone on with the infantry. He had been the last to leave the tank, and as he had stepped out to the ground, a shell exploded directly beneath him, taking off both of his legs below the knee.

The last of the tanks waddled wearily in and the work of checking-up began. All were accounted for but two. Their fate still remains a secret. Our theory was that they had gone too far ahead and had entered the village in back of the German lines; that the infantry had not been able to keep up with them, and that they had been captured. Two or three days afterwards an airman told us that he had seen, on the day of the battle, two tanks far ahead of the infantry and that they appeared to be stranded.

Weeks later we attacked at the point where the tanks had been, and on some German prisoners whom we took, we found several photographs of these identical tanks. Then one day, when we had stopped wondering about them, a sergeant in our company received a letter from one of the crew of the missing machines, saying that he was a prisoner in Germany. But of the officers we have never heard to this day.

We sat around wearily, waiting for the motor lorries which were to take some of us back to B———. Years seemed to have been crowded into the hours that had elapsed. Talbot glanced at his watch. It was still only eight o'clock in the morning. Again he experienced the feeling of incredulity that comes to one who has had much happen in the hours between dawn and early morning and who discovers that the day has but just begun. He had thought it must be three o'clock in the afternoon, at least. The lorries arrived eventually, and took those who had no tanks, back to B———. The others brought the "Willies" in by the evening.

CHAPTER 7

The Second Battle

Ten days had now elapsed since that day when we had gone back to B—— with the officers and men who had survived. We had enjoyed every minute of our rest and once more were feeling fit. The remainder of the Company had been divided up into crews. The "Willies" themselves had had the best of care and attention.

Most important of all, to the childish minds of that part of the British Army which we represented, we had given another concert which had been an even greater success than the first. The Old Bird and Berwick had excelled themselves. We were convinced that something was wrong with a Government that would send two such artists to the front! They should be at home, writing "words and music" that would live forever.

Toward the end of the week, plans for another attack were arranged. This time it was to take place at C——, about five miles north of N——. We were told that this was to be a "big show" at last. Part of the Hindenburg Line had been taken, and part was still in the hands of the enemy. It had been decided, therefore, that this sector of the line, and the village behind it, must be captured. Our share in the business consisted of a few tanks to work with the infantry.

Two of us went up three days before to arrange the plans with the divisional commander. We wandered up into the Hindenburg Line as close as we could get to the Boche, to see what the ground was like, and to decide if possible on the routes for the tanks. In the line were innumerable souvenirs. We found the furniture that the Germans had taken out of the villages on their retirement, and had used to make their line more comfortable.

We found, too, an extraordinary piece of engineering. A tunnel about ten miles long ran underneath the whole of the Hindenburg Line. It was about thirty or forty feet down, and had been dug, we heard, by Russian prisoners. The tunnel was about six feet wide and about five feet high. It had been roughly balked in with timber, and at every twenty yards, a shaft led out of the tunnel up into the trench. Berwick found a large mirror which he felt could not be wasted under the circumstances. He could not resist its charm, so he started lugging it back the six miles to camp. It was very heavy and its charm had decreased greatly by the time he reached camp and found that no one could make any use of it.

The day of the attack was still undecided, and in order to be quite ready when it should come off, we left B—— with the tanks one evening and took them up to Saint-L——, a little place about three thousand yards away from the Hindenburg Line. Here we staged them behind a railway embankment, underneath a bridge that had been partially blown up. This was the same embankment, as a matter of fact, behind which, four or five miles away, the Australian dressing-station had been established in the last battle.

Here we spent two or three days tuning up the machines, and many of our leisure moments in watching a howitzer battery which was just beside us. This was fascinating. If you stand by the gun when it is fired, you can see the shell leave the muzzle, and watch the black mass shoot its seven or eight thousand yards until it becomes a small speck and finally vanishes just before it hits the ground.

We also made an interesting collection of German and English shell-cases. These cases are made of brass, and the four-fives, especially, in the opinion of some people, make very nice rose-bowls when they are polished, with wire arranged inside to hold the blossoms. Weird music could be heard issuing from our dugout at times, when we gave an impromptu concert, by putting several of these shell-cases on a log of wood and playing elaborate tunes on them with a bit of stone.

All this merry-making came to an end, though. One day we received word that the attack was to come off the next morning. Then began the preparations in earnest and the day went with a rush. At this part of the Hindenburg Line, it was very easy to lose one's way, especially at night. The tanks were scheduled to start moving up at ten o'clock. Talbot and the Old Bird, with several men, set out at about eight, and arranged for marks to guide the machines.

We had just reached a part of the Hindenburg Line which was now in our possession, and were near an ammunition dump, when shells began to fall around us. They were not near enough to do us any harm, and we continued our work, when one dropped into the ammunition dump and exploded. In an instant the whole dump was alight. It was like some terrible and giant display of pyrotechnics. Gas shells, Verey lights, and stink bombs filled the air with their nauseous odours. Shells of all sizes blew up and fell in steely splinters. The noise was deafening. Cursing our luck, we waited until it died down into a red, smouldering mass, and then edged up cautiously to continue our work. By this time, Berwick's tank came up, and he emerged, with a broad smile on his face.

"Having a good time?" he asked genially.

There was a frozen silence, excepting for his inane laughter. He made a few more irritating remarks which he seemed to think were very funny, and then he disappeared inside his tank and prepared to follow us. We had gone ahead a couple of hundred yards when we heard bombs exploding, and looking back we saw the tank standing still, with fireworks going off under one of her tracks.

Presently the noise ceased, and after waiting a moment we strolled back. As we reached the tank, Berwick and the crew came tumbling out, making the air blue with their language. They had run over a box of bombs, the only thing that had survived the fire in the ammunition dump, and one of the tracks was damaged. To repair it meant several hours' hard work in the cold in unpleasant proximity to the still smouldering dump. Over Talbot's face spread a broad smile.

"Having a good time?" he asked pleasantly of Berwick.

Infuriated growls were his only answer. He moved on with his men, while Berwick and his crew settled down to work.

The night was fortunately dark. They went slowly forward and brought the route almost up to within calling distance of the Germans. The Verey lights, shattering the darkness over No Man's Land, did not disclose them to the enemy. Suddenly, a Boche machine gun mechanically turned its attentions toward the place where they were working. With a tightening of every muscle, Talbot heard the slow whisper of the gun.

As it turned to sweep the intervening space between the lines, the whisper rose to a shirring hiss. The men dropped to the ground, flattening themselves into the earth. But Talbot stood still. Now, if ever, was the time when an example would count. If they all dropped to the ground every time a machine gun rattled, the job would never be done. So, hands in his pockets, but with awful "wind up," he waited while the soft patter of the bullets came near and the patter quickened into rain. As it reached him, the rain became a fierce torrent, stinging the top of the parapet behind them as the bullets tore by viciously a few inches above his head.

Then as it passed, it dropped into a patter once more and finally dropped away in a whisper. Talbot suddenly realized that his throat was aching, but that he was untouched by the storm. The men slowly got to their feet and continued their work in silence. Although the machine gun continued to spatter bullets near them all through the hours they were working, not once again did the men drop when they heard the whisper begin. The job was finally done and they filed wearily back.

The attack was timed to come off at dawn. An hour before, while it was still as black as pitch, the tanks moved again for their final starting-point. McKnutt's machine was the first to go.

"Cheero, McKnutt," we said as he clambered in. "Good luck!"

The men followed, some through the top and some through the side. The doors and portholes were closed, and in a moment the exhaust began to puff merrily. The tank crawled forward and soon disappeared into the blackness.

She had about fifteen hundred yards to go, parallel with the Hindenburg Line, and several trenches to cross before coming up with the enemy. We had planned that the tanks would take about three quarters of an hour to reach their starting-point, and that soon after they arrived there, the show would begin.

Since it was still dark and the attack had not commenced, McKnutt and his first driver opened the windows in front of them. They looked out into impenetrable gloom. It was necessary to turn their headlights on, and with this help, they crawled along a little more securely. A signal from the driver, and they got into top gear. She bumped along, over shell-holes and mine-craters at the exhilarating speed of about four miles an hour, and then arrived at the first trench to be crossed. It was about ten feet wide with high banks on each side.

"One up!" signals the driver. The gears-men get into first gear, and the tank tilts back as it goes up one side of the trench. Suddenly she starts tipping over, and the driver takes out his clutch and puts on his brake hard.

McKnutt yells out, "Hold tight!" and the tank slides gently down with her nose in the bottom of the trench. The driver lets in his clutch again, the tank digs her nose into the other side and pulls herself up slowly, while her tail dips down into the bottom of the trench. Then comes the great strain as she pulls herself bodily out of the trench until she balances on the far side.

It was now no longer safe to run with lights. They were snapped off. Once more the darkness closed around them, blacker than ever. They could no longer find their route, and McKnutt jumped out, walking ahead with the tank lumbering along behind. Twice he lost his way and they were obliged to wait until he found it again. Then, to his intense relief, the moon shone out with a feeble light. It was just enough to illumine faintly the ground before them and McKnutt re-entered the tank, and started on.

Their route ran close to the sides of an old quarry and they edged along cautiously. McKnutt, with his eyes glued to the front, decided that they must have already passed the end of the quarry. That would mean that they were not far from the spot where they were to wait for the signal to go into action. The moon had again disappeared behind the clouds, but he did not consider it worthwhile to get out again. The journey would be over in a few minutes.

Suddenly, his heart took a great dive and he seemed to stop breathing. He felt the tank balance ever so slightly. Staring with aching eyes through the portholes, he saw that they were on the edge of the old quarry, with a forty-foot drop down its steep sides before them. The black depth seemed bottomless. The tank was slipping over. When she shot down they would all be killed from concussion alone.

His heart was pounding so that he could hardly speak. But the driver, too, had seen the danger.

"For God's sake, take out your clutch and put your brake on!" McKnutt yelled, his voice almost drowned by the rattle and roar inside the tank. The man kept his head. As the tail of the tank started tipping up, he managed somehow with the brakes to hold her on the edge. For a second or two, she swayed there. She seemed to be unable to decide whether to kill them or not. The slightest crumbling of the earth or the faintest out-side movement against the tank would precipitate them over the edge. The brakes would not hold them for long. Then the driver acted. Slowly he put his gears in reverse, keeping the brake on hard until the engine had taken up the strain. Slowly she moved back until her tail bumped on the ground, and she settled down. Neither McKnutt nor his driver spoke. They pushed back their tin hats and wiped their foreheads.

McKnutt glanced back at the men in the rear of the tank. They, of course, had been unable to see out, and had no idea of what they had escaped. Now that the danger was passed, he felt an unreasonable annoyance that none of them would ever know what he and the driver had gone through in those few moments. Then the feeling passed, he signalled, "Neutral left," the gearsman locked his left track, and the tank swung over, passing safely by the perilous spot.

They settled down now to a snail's pace, shutting off their engine, as the Germans could not be more than one hundred and fifty or two hundred yards away. Running at full speed, the engine would have been heard by them. In a few moments, they arrived at their appointed station. McKnutt glanced at his watch. They had only a few moments to wait. The engine was shut off and they stopped.

The heat inside the tank was oppressive. McKnutt and James opened the top, and crawled out, the men following. They looked around. The first streaks of light were beginning to show in the sky. A heavy silence hung over everything—the silence that always precedes a bombardment. Presumably, only the attacking forces feel this. Even the desultory firing seems to have faded away. All the little ordinary noises have ceased. It is a sickening quiet, so loud in itself that it makes one's heart beat quicker. It is because one is listening so intensely for the guns to break out that all other sounds have lost their significance. One seems to have become all ears—to have no sense of sight or touch or taste or smell. All seem to have become merged in the sense of hearing. The very air itself seems tense with listening. Only the occasional rattle of a machine gun breaks the stillness. Even this passes unnoticed.

Slowly the minute-hand crept round to the half-hour, and the men slipped back into their steel home. Doors were bolted and portholes shut, save for the tiny slits in front of officer and driver, through which they peered. The engine was ready to start. The petrol was on and flooding. They waited quietly. Their heavy breathing was the only sound. The minute-hand reached the half-hour.

With the crash and swish of thousands of shells, the guns

smashed the stillness. Instantly, the flash of their explosion lit up the opposite trenches. For a fraction of a second the thought came to McKnutt how wonderful it was that man could produce a sound to which Nature had no equal, either in violence or intensity. But the time was for action and not for reflection.

"Start her up!" yelled out McKnutt.

But the engine would not fire.

"What the devil's the matter?" cried James.

A bit of tinkering with the carburettor, and the engine purred softly. Its noise was drowned in the pandemonium raging around them. James let in the clutch, and the monster moved forward on her errand of destruction.

Although it was not light enough to distinguish forms, the flashes of the shell-fire and the bursts from the shrapnel lit up that part of the Hindenburg Line that lay on the other side of the barrier. One hundred and fifty yards, and the tank was almost on top of the barricade. Bombs were exploding on both sides. McKnutt slammed down the shutters of the portholes in front of him and his driver. "Bullets," he said shortly.

"One came through, I think, sir," James replied. With the portholes shut, there was no chance for bullets to enter now through the little pin-points directly above the slits in the shutters. In order to see through these, it is necessary to place one's eye directly against the cold metal. They are safe, for if a bullet does hit them, it cannot come through, although it may stop up the hole.

Suddenly a dull explosion was heard on the roof of the tank.

"They're bombing us, sir!" cried one of the gunners. McKnutt signalled to him, and he opened fire from his sponson. They plunged along, amid a hail of bullets, while bombs exploded all around them.

McKnutt and James, with that instinctive sense of direction which comes to men who control these machines, felt that they were hovering on the edge of the German trench. Then a sudden flash from the explosion of a huge shell lit up the ground around them, and they saw four or five gray-clad figures, about ten yards away, standing on the parapet hysterically hurling bombs at the machine. They might as well have been throwing pebbles. Scornfully the tank slid over into the wide trench and landed with a crash in the bottom. For a moment she lay there without moving. The Germans thought she was stuck. They came running along thinking to grapple with her. But they never reached her, for at once the guns from both sides opened fire and the Germans disappeared.

The huge machine dragged herself up the steep ten-foot side of the trench. As she neared the top, it seemed as if the engine would not take the final pull. James took out his clutch, put his brake on hard, and raced the engine. Then letting the clutch in with a jerk, the tank pulled herself right on to the point of balance, and tipped slowly over what had been the parapet of the German position.

Now she was in the wire which lay in front of the trench. McKnutt signalled back, "Swing round to the left," parallel to the lay of the line. A moment's pause, and she moved forward relentlessly, crushing everything in her path, and sending out a stream of bullets from every turret to any of the enemy who dared to show themselves above the top of the trench.

At the same time our own troops, who had waited behind the barricade to bomb their way down, from traverse to traverse, rushed over the heap of sandbags, tangled wire, wood, and dead men which barred their way. The moral effect of the tank's success, and the terror which she inspired, cheered our infantry on to greater efforts. The tank crew were, at the time, unaware of the infantry's action, as none of our own men could be seen. The only indication of the fact was the bursting of the bombs which gradually moved from fire bay to fire bay.

The corporal touched McKnutt on the arm.

"I don't believe our people are keeping up with us, sir," he said. "They seem to have been stopped about thirty yards back."

"All right," McKnutt answered. "We'll turn round."

McKnutt and James opened their portholes to obtain a clearer view. Five yards along to the left, a group of Germans were holding up the advancing British. They had evidently prepared a barricade in case of a possible bombing attack on our part, and this obstacle, together with a fusillade of bombs which met them, prevented our troops from pushing on.

McKnutt seized his gun and pushed it through the mounting, but found that he could not swing round far enough to get an aim on the enemy. But James was in a better position. He picked the gray figures off, one by one, until the bombing ceased and our own men jumped over the barricade and came down among the dead and wounded Germans.

Then a sudden and unexplainable sense of disaster caused McKnutt to look round. One of his gunners lay quite still on the floor of the tank, his back against the engine, and a stream of blood trickling down his face. The corporal who stood next to him pointed to the sights in the turret and then to his forehead, and McKnutt realized that a bullet must have slipped in through the small space, entering the man's head as he looked along the barrel of his gun. There he lay, along one side of the tank between the engine and the sponson. The corporal tried to get in position to carry on firing with his own gun, but the dead body impeded his movements.

There was only one thing to do. The corporal looked questioningly at McKnutt and pointed to the body. The officer nodded quickly, and the left gears-man and the corporal dragged the body and propped it up against the door. Immediately the door flew open. The back of the corpse fell down and half the body lay hanging out, with its legs still caught on the floor. With feverish haste they lifted the legs and threw them out, but the weight of the body balanced them back again through the still open door.

The men were desperate. With a tremendous heave they turned the dead man upside down, shoved the body out and slammed the door shut. They were just in time. A bomb exploded directly beneath the sponson, where the dead body had fallen. To every man in the tank came a feeling of swift gratitude that the bombs had caught the dead man and not themselves.

They ploughed across another trench without dropping into the bottom, for it was only six feet wide. Daylight had come by now and the enemy was beginning to find that his brave efforts were of no avail against these monsters of steel.

All this time the German guns had not been silent. McKnutt's tank crunched across the ground amid a furious storm of flying earth and splinters. The strain was beginning to be felt. Although one is protected from machine-gun fire in a tank, the sense of confinement is, at times, terrible. One does not know what is happening outside his little steel prison. One often cannot see where the machine is going. The noise inside is deafening; the heat terrific. Bombs shatter on the roof and on all sides. Bullets spatter savagely against the walls.

There is an awful lack of knowledge; a feeling of blind helplessness at being cooped up. One is entirely at the mercy of the big shells. If a shell hits a tank near the petrol tank, the men may perish by fire, as did Gould, without a chance of escape. Going down with your ship seems pleasant compared to burning up with your tank. In fighting in the open, one has, at least, air and space.

McKnutt, however, was lucky. They could now see the sunken road before them which was their objective. Five-nines were dropping around them now. It was only a matter of moments, it seemed, when they would be struck.

"Do you think we shall make it?" McKnutt asked James.

"We may get there, but shall we get back? That's the question, sir."

McKnutt did not answer. They had both had over two years' experience of the accuracy of the German artillery. And they did not believe in miracles. But they had their orders. They must simply do their duty and trust to luck.

They reached the sunken road. The tank was swung around. Their orders were to reach their objective and remain there until the bombers arrived. McKnutt peered out. No British were in sight, and he snapped his porthole shut. Grimly they settled down to wait.

A TANK BRINGING IN A CAPTURED GERMAN GUN UNDER PROTECTION OF CAMOUFLAGE

The moments passed. Each one seemed as if it would be their last. Would the infantry never come? Would there be any sense in just sitting there until a German shell annihilated them if the infantry never arrived? Had they been pushed back by a German rush? Should he take it upon himself to turn back? McKnutt's brain whirled.

Then, after hours, it seemed, of waiting, around the corner of a traverse, he saw one of the British tin hats. Nothing in the world could have been a happier sight. A great wave of relief swept over him. Three or four more appeared. Realizing that they, too, had reached their objective, they stopped and began to throw up a rough form of barricade. More men poured in. The position was consolidated, and there was nothing more for the tank to do.

They swung round and started back. Two shells dropped about twenty yards in front of them. For a moment McKnutt wondered whether it would be well to change their direction. "No, we'll keep right on and chance it," he said aloud. The next moment a tremendous crash seemed to lift the tank off the ground. Black smoke and flying particles filled the tank. McKnutt and James looked around expecting to see the top of the machine blown off. But nothing had happened inside, and no one was injured. Although shells continued to fall around them and a German machine gun raged at them, they got back safely.

Brigade Headquarters, where McKnutt reported, was full of expectancy. Messages were pouring in over the wires. The men at the telephones were dead beat, but cool and collected.

"Any news of the other 'busses?" McKnutt asked eagerly. The Buzzers shook their heads wearily. He rushed up to a couple of men who were being carried to a dressing-station.

"Do you fellows know how the tanks made out?" he asked.

One of them had seen two of the machines on the other side of the German line, he said. In answer to the questions which were fired at him he could only say that the tanks had pushed on beyond the German front line.

Then on the top of the hill, against the skyline, they saw a little group of three or four men. James recognized them.

"Why, there's Sergeant Browning and Mr. Berwick, sir," he said. "What's happened to their tank, I wonder?" He and McKnutt hurried over to meet them.

Berwick smiled coolly.

"Hullo!" he said in his casual manner.

"What's happened to your 'bus?" "What did you do?" was fired at him.

"We got stuck in the German wire, and the infantry got ahead of us," he said. "We pushed on, and fell into a nest of three machine guns. They couldn't hurt us, of course, and the Boches finally ran away. We knocked out about ten of them, and just as we were going on and were already moving, we suddenly started twisting around in circles. What do you think had happened? A trench mortar had got us full in one of our tracks, and the beastly thing broke. So we all tumbled out and left her there."

"Didn't you go on with the infantry?" asked McKnutt.

"No. They'd reached their objective by that time," Berwick replied, "so we saved the tank guns, and I pinched the clock. Then we strolled back, and here we are," he concluded.

Talbot joined the group as he finished.

" But where's the rest of your crew? " he asked.

Berwick said quietly: "Jameson and Corporal Fiske got knocked out coming back." He lit a cigarette and puffed at it.

There was silence for a moment.

Then Talbot said, "Bad luck; have you got their pay-books?"

"No, I forgot them," Berwick answered.

But his sergeant handed over the little brown books which were the only tangible remains of two men who had gone into action that morning. The pay-books contained two or three pages on which were jotted down their pay, with the officer's signature. They had been used as pocket-books, and held a few odd letters which the men had received a few days before. Talbot had often been given the pay-books of men in his company who were killed, but he never failed to be affected when he discovered the letters and little trifles which had meant so much to the men who had carried them, and which now would mean so much to those whom they had left behind.

In silence they went back to McKnutt's tank and sat down, waiting for news. Scraps of information were beginning to trickle in.

"Have gained our objective in X Wood. Have not been counter-attacked."

"Cannot push on owing to heavy machine-gun fire from C——."

"Holding out with twenty men in trench running north from Derelict Wood. Can I have reinforcements?"

These were the messages pouring in from different points on the lines of attack. Sometimes the messages came in twos and threes. Sometimes there were minutes when only a wild buzzing could be heard and the men at the telephones tried to make the buzzing intelligible.

The situation cleared up finally, however. Our troops had, apparently, gained their objectives along the entire line to the right. On the left the next brigade had been hung up by devastating machine-gun fire. As McKnutt and Talbot waited around for news and fresh orders, one of their men hurried down and saluted.

He brought the news that the other three tanks had returned, having reached their objectives. Two had but little opposition and the infantry had found no difficulty in gaining their points of attack. The third tank, however, had had three men wounded at a "pill-box." These pill-boxes are little concrete forts which the German had planted along his line. The walls are of ferro concrete, two to three feet thick. As the tank reached the pill-box, two Germans slipped out of the rear door. Three of the tank crew clambered down and got inside the pill-box.

In a moment the firing from inside ceased, and presently the door flew open. Two British tank men, dirty and grimy, escorting ten Germans, filed out. The Germans had their hands above their heads, and when ordered to the rear they went with the greatest alacrity. One of the three Englishmen was badly wounded; the other two were only slightly injured, but they wandered down to the dressing-station, with the hope that "Blighty" would soon welcome them.

Although Talbot had his orders to hold the tanks in readiness in case they were needed, no necessity arose, and after a few hours' waiting, the major sent word to him to start the tanks back to the embankment, there to be kept for the next occasion. Better still, the men were to be taken back to B—— in the motor lorries, just as they had been after the first battle. Water, comparative quiet, blankets, these were the luxuries that lay before them.

As he sat crowded into the swaying motor lorry that lurched back along the shell-torn road to B——, Talbot slipped his hand into his pocket. He touched a cheque-book, a package of cigarettes, and a razor. Then he smiled. They were the final preparations he had made that morning before he went into action. After all he had not needed them, but one never could tell, one might be taken prisoner. One needed no such material preparations against the possibility of death, but a prisoner—that was different.

The cheque-book had been for use in a possible gray prison camp in the land of his enemies. Cheques would some time or other reach his English bank and his people would know that he was, at least, alive. The cigarettes were to keep up his courage in the face of whatever disaster might befall him.

And the razor? Most important of all.

The razor was to keep, bright and untarnished, the traditions and prestige of the British Army!

CHAPTER 8

Rest and Discipline

We stayed in that region of the Front for a few more weeks, preparing for any other task that might be demanded of us. One day the battalion received its orders to pack up, to load the tanks that were left over, and to be ready for its return to the district in which we had spent the winter.

We entrained on a Saturday evening at A——, and arrived at St.-P—— at about ten o'clock on Sunday night. From there a twelve-mile march lay before us to our old billets in B——. As may well be imagined, the men, though tired, were in high spirits. We simply ate up the distance, and the troops disguised their fatigue by singing songs. There were two which appeared to be favourites on this occasion.

One, to the tune of "The Church's One Foundation," ran as follows:—

We are Fred Karno's [1] Army,
The ragtime A.S.C., [2]
We cannot work, we do not fight,
So what ruddy use are we?
And when we get to Berlin,
The Kaiser he will say,
Hoch, hoch, mein Gott!
What a ruddy rotten lot,

---

1. A late, third-rate English pantomime producer.
2. Stands for Army Service Corps, and its equivalent in the American Army is the Quartermaster's Corps.

Is the ragtime A.S.C.

The other was a refrain to the tune of a Salvation Army hymn, "When the Roll is called up Yonder":—

When you wash us in the water,
That you washed your dirty daughter,
Oh! then we will be much whiter!
We'll be whiter than the whitewash on the wall.

Eventually the companies arrived in the village at all hours of the morning. No one was up. We saw that the men received their meals, which had been prepared by the cooks who had gone ahead in motor lorries. They did not spend much time over the food, for in less than half an hour "K" billets—the same Hospice de Ste. Berthe—were perfectly quiet.

We then wandered away with our servants, to be met at each of our houses by hastily clad landladies, with sleep in their eyes and smoking lamps or guttering candles in their hands.

The next morning the company paraded at half-past nine, and the day was spent in re-forming sections, in issuing new kits to the men, and in working the rosters for the various courses. On Tuesday, just as breakfast was starting, an orderly brought a couple of memorandums from Battalion Orderly Room for McKnutt and Berwick.

No one watched them read the chits, but Talbot, glancing up from his plate, saw a look on Berwick's face. It was a look of the purest joy.

"What is it?" he said.

"Leave, my God!" replied Berwick; "and McKnutt 's got it too."

"When are you going? Today?" shouted the Old Bird.

"Yes; there's a car to take us to the station in a quarter of an hour."

They both left their unfinished breakfasts and tore off to their billets. There it was but a matter of moments to throw a few things into their packs. No one ever takes any luggage when going on leave. They tore back to the mess to leave instructions

A British tank in the Liberty Loan Parade in New York

for their servants, and we strolled out *en masse* to see the lucky fellows off.

The box-body drew away from where we were standing. We watched it grow smaller and smaller down the long white road, and turned back with regrets and pleasure in our hearts. With regrets, that we ourselves were not the lucky ones, and knowing that for some of us leave would never come; with pleasure, because one is always glad that a few of the deserving reap a small share of their reward.

Then, strolling over to the Parade Ground, we heard the "Five Minutes" sounding. Some dashed off to get their Sam Brownes, others called for their servants to wipe a few flecks of dust from their boots and puttees.

When the "Fall In" began, the entire company was standing "At Ease" on the Parade Ground. As the last note of the call sounded, the whole parade sprang to "Attention," and the major, who had been standing on the edge of the field, walked forward to inspect.

Every morning was spent in this manner, except for those who had special courses to follow. We devoted all our time and attention to "Forming Fours" in as perfect a manner as possible; to saluting with the greatest accuracy and fierceness; and to unwearying repetition of every movement and detail, until machine-like precision was attained.

All that we were doing then is the very foundation and essence of good discipline. Discipline is the state to which a man is trained, in order that under all circumstances he shall carry out without secondary reasoning any order that may be given him by a superior. There is nothing of a servile nature in this form of obedience. Each man realizes that it is for the good of the whole. By placing his implicit confidence in the commands of one of a higher rank than his own, he gives an earnest of his ability to himself command at some future time. It is but another proof of the old adage, that the man who obeys least is the least fitted to command.

When this war started, certain large formations, with the sheer lust for fighting in their blood, did not, while being formed, realize the absolute necessity of unending drill and inspection. Their first cry was, "Give us a rifle, a bayonet, and a bomb, show us how to use them, and we will do the rest."

Acting upon this idea, they flung themselves into battle, disregarding the iron rules of a preliminary training. At first their very impetus and courage carried them over incredible obstacles. But after a time, and as their best were killed off, the original blaze died down, and the steady flame of ingrained discipline was not there to take the place of burning enthusiasm. The terrible waste and useless sacrifice that ensued showed only too plainly that even the greatest individual bravery is not enough.

In this modern warfare there are many trials and experiences unimagined before, which wear down the actual will-power of the men who undergo them. When troops are forced to sit in a trench under the most terrific shell-fire, the nerve-racking noise, the sight of their comrades and their defences being blown to atoms, and the constant fear that they themselves will be the next to go, all deprive the ordinary mind of vital initiative. Having lost the active mental powers that a human being possesses, they are reduced to the level of machines.

The officers and non-commissioned officers, on whom the responsibility of leadership rests, have that spur to maintain their equilibrium, but the private soldiers, who have themselves only to think of, are the most open to this devastating influence. If these machines are to be controlled, as they must be, by an exterior intelligence, they must obey automatically, and if in the past automatic obedience has not been implanted, there is nothing to take its place.

The only means by which to obtain inherent response to a given order is so to train a man in minute details, by constant, inflexible insistence on perfection, that it becomes part of his being to obey without thinking.

It must not be presumed that, in obtaining this almost inhuman reaction, all independent qualities are obliterated. For, though a man's mind is adjusted to carrying out, without questioning, any task that is demanded of him, yet in the execution of this duty he is allowed the full scope of his invention and initiative.

Thus, by this dull and unending routine, we laid the foundation of that inevitable success toward which we were slowly working.

When the company dismissed, the major, Talbot, and the Old Bird walked over to lunch together.

"Well, it's a great war, isn't it?" said the major, turning to the other two.

"It's very nice to have got through a couple of shows, sir," replied Talbot. "What do you think about it, Old Bird?"

"Well, of course, war is all very well for those who like it. But give me the Base every time," answered the Old Bird, true to his reputation. Then, turning to the major with his most ingratiating smile, he said, "By the way, sir, what about a few days in Boulogne?"

CHAPTER 9

A Philosophy of War

It has often been observed that if this war is to end war for all time, and if all the sacrifices and misery and suffering will help to prevent any recurrence of them, then it is well worth while.

In these days of immediate demands and quick results, this question is too vague and too far-reaching to bring instant consolation. Apart from that, too, it cannot decide whether any war, however great, can ever abolish the natural and primitive fighting instinct in man. The source from which we must draw the justification for our optimism lies much nearer to hand. We must regard the effect that warring life has already produced upon each individual member of the nations who are and who are not engaged in it.

At the very heart of it is the effect on the man who is actually fighting. Take the case of him who before the war was either working in a factory, who was a clerk in a business house, or who was nothing at all beyond the veriest loafer and bar-lounger. To begin with, he was perhaps purely selfish. The foundation of his normal life was self-protection. Whether worthless or worthy, whether hating or respecting his superiors, the private gain and comfort for himself and his was the object of his existence. He becomes a soldier, and that act alone is a conversion.

His wife and children are cared for, it is true; but he himself, for a shilling a day, sells to his country his life, his health, his pleasures, and his hopes for the future. To make good measure he throws in cheerfulness, devotion, philosophy, humour, and an unfailing kindness. One man, for instance, sells up three grocery businesses in the heart of Lancashire, an ambition which it has taken him ten years to accomplish. Without a trace of bitterness he divorces himself from the routine of a lifetime, and goes out to France to begin life again at the very bottom of a new ladder. He who for years had many men under him is now under all, and receives, unquestioningly, orders which in a different sphere he had been accustomed to give.

Apart from the mere letter of obedience and discipline he gains a spirit of devotion and self-sacrifice, which turns the bare military instrument into a divine virtue. He may, for instance, take up the duties of an officer's servant. Immediately he throws himself whole-heartedly into a new form of selfless generosity, which leads him to a thousand ways of care and forethought, that even the tenderest woman could hardly conceive. The man who receives this unwavering devotion can only accept it with the knowledge that no one can deserve it, and that it is greater gain to him who gives than to him who takes.

What life of peace is there that produces this god-like fibre in the plainest of men? Why, indeed, is it produced in the life of war? It is because in war sordidness and petty worries are eliminated; because the one great and ever-present fear, the fear of death, reduces all other considerations to their proper values. The actual fear of death is always present, but this fear itself cannot be sordid when men can meet it of their own free will and with the most total absence of cringing or of cowardice.

In commercial rivalry a man will sacrifice the friend of years to gain a given sum, which will insure him increased material comforts. In war a man will deliberately sacrifice the life for which he wanted those comforts, to save perhaps a couple of men who have no claim on him whatsoever. He who before feared any household calamity now throws himself upon a live bomb, which, even though he might escape himself, will without his action kill other men who are near it. This deed loses none of its value because of the general belief among soldiers that life is cheap. Other men's lives are cheap. One's own life is always very dear.

One of the most precious results has been the resurrection of the quality of admiration. The man who before the war said, "Why is he my master?" is now only too glad to accept a leader who is a leader indeed. He has learned that as his leader cannot do without him, so he cannot do without his leader, and although each is of equal importance in the scheme of affairs, their positions in the scheme are different. He has learned that there is a higher equality than the equality of class: it is the equality of spirit.

This same feeling is reflected, more especially among the leaders of the men, in the complete disappearance of snobbishness. No such artificial imposition can survive in a life where inherent value automatically finds its level; where a disguise which in peace-time passed as superiority, now disintegrates when in contact with this life of essentials. For war is, above all, a reduction to essentials. It is the touchstone which proves the qualities of our youth's training. All those pleasures that formed the gamut of a young man's life either fall away completely or find their proper place. Sport, games, the open-air life, have taught him that high cheerfulness, through failure or success, which makes endurance possible.

But the complicated, artificial pleasures of ordinary times have receded into a dim, unspoken background. The wholesomeness of the existence that he now leads has taught him to delight in the most simple and natural of things. This throwing aside of the perversions and fripperies of an over-civilization has forced him to regard them with a disgust that can never allow him to be tempted again by their inducements of delight and dissipation.

The natural, healthy desires which a man is sometimes inclined to indulge in are no longer veiled under a mask of hypocrisy. They are treated in a perfectly outspoken fashion as the necessary accompaniments to a hard, open-air life, where a man's vitality is at its best. In consequence of this, and as the result of the deepening of man's character which war inevitably produces, the sense of adventure and mystery which accompanied the fulfilment of these desires has disappeared, and with it to a great extent the desires themselves have assumed a far less importance.

In peace, and especially in war, the young man's creed is casualness. Not the casualness of carelessness, but that which comes from the knowledge that up to each given point he has done his best. It is this fundamental peace of mind which comes to a soldier that forms the beauty of his life. The order received must be obeyed in its exact degree, neither more nor less; and the responsibility, though great, is clearly denned. Each man must use his individual intelligence within the scope of the part assigned to him.

The responsibility differs in kind, but not in degree, and the last link of the chain is as important as the first. There can be no shirking or shifting, and, knowing this, each task is finished, rounded out, and put away. One might think that this made thought mechanical: but it is mechanical only in so far as each man's intelligence is concentrated on his own particular duty, and each part working in perfect order contributes to the unison through which the whole machine develops its power. Thus the military life induces in men a clearer and more accurate habit of thought, and teaches each one to do his work well and above all to do his own work only.

From this very simplicity of life, which brings out a calmness of mind and that equable temperament that minor worries can no longer shake, springs the mental leisure which gives time for other and unaccustomed ideas. Men who wittingly, time and again, have faced but escaped death, will inevitably begin to think what death may mean. As the first lessons of obedience teach each man that he needs a leader to pass through a certain crisis, so the crisis of death, where man must pass alone, demands a still higher Leader.

With the admission that no man is self-sufficient, that sin of pride, which is the strongest barrier between a man and his God, falls away. He is forced, if only in self-defence, to recognize that faith in some all-sufficient Power is the only thing that will carry him through. If he could cut away the thousand sins of thought, man would automatically find himself at faith. It is the central but often hidden point of our intelligence; and although there are a hundred roads that lead to it, they may be completely blocked. The clean flame of the disciplined life burns away the rubbish that chokes these roads, and faith becomes a nearer and more constant thing. The sadness of war lies in the loss of actual personalities, but it is only by means of these losses that this surrender can be attained.

It must not be thought that faith comes overnight as a free gift. It is a long and slow process of many difficult steps. There may be first the actual literal crumbling, unknown in peacetime, of one's solid surroundings, to be repeated perhaps again and again until the old habit of reliance upon them is uprooted. Then comes the realization that this life at the front has but two possible endings. The first is to be so disabled that a man's fighting days are over. The other is death. Instant death rather than a slow death from wounds. Every man hopes for a wound which will send him home to England.

That, however, is only a respite, as his return to France follows upon his convalescence. The other most important step is the loss of one's friends. It is not the fact of actually seeing them killed, for in the chaos and tumult of a battle the mind hardly registers such impressions. One's only feeling is the purely primitive one of relief, that it is another and not one's self. It is only afterwards, when the excitement is over, and a man realizes that again there is a space of life, for him, but not for his friend, that the loneliness and the loss are felt. He then says to himself, "Why am I spared when many better men have gone?"

At first resentment swallows up all other emotions. In time, when this bitterness begins to pass, the belief that somehow this loss is of some avail, carries him a little farther on the road to faith. This all comes to the man who before the war believed that the world was made for his pleasure, and who treated life from that standpoint. All that he wanted he took without asking.

Now, all that he has he gives without being asked.

Woman, too, gives more than herself. She gives her men, her peace of mind and all that makes her life worth living. The man after all may have little hope, but while he is alive he has the daily pleasures of health, vitality, excitement, and a thousand interests. A woman has but a choice of sorrows: the sorrow of unbearable suspense or the acceptance of the end.

Yet it needed this war to show again to women what they could best do in life: to love their men, bear their children, care for the sick and suffering, and learn to endure. It has taught them also to accept from man what he is able or willing to give, and to admit a higher claim than their own. They have been forced to put aside the demands and exactions which they felt before were their right, and to accept loneliness and loss without murmur or question.

A woman who loses her son loses the supreme reason of her existence; and yet the day after the news has come, she goes back to her work for the sons of other women. If she has more sons to give she gives them, and faces again the eternal suspense that she has lived through before. The younger women, who in times of peace would have looked forward to an advantageous and comfortable marriage, will now marry men whom they may never see again after the ten days' honeymoon is over, and will unselfishly face the very real possibility of widowhood and lonely motherhood. They have had to learn the old lesson that work for others is the only cure for sorrow, and they have learned too that it is the only cure for all those petty worries and boredoms which assailed them in times of peace. If they have learned this, then again one may say that war is worthwhile.

What effect has the war had upon those countries who in the beginning were not engaged in it? The United States, for instance, has for three years been an onlooker. The people of that country have had every opportunity to view, in their proper perspectives, the feelings and changes brought about among the men and women of the combatant countries.

At first, the enormous casualties, the sufferings and the sorrow, led them to believe that nothing was worth the price they would have to pay, were they to enter into the lists. For in the beginning, before that wonderful philosophy of spirit and cheerfulness of outlook arose, and before the far-reaching effects of the sacrifice of loved ones could be perceived, there seemed to be little reason or right for such a train of desolation. They were perfectly justified, too, in thinking this, when insufficient time had elapsed to enable them to judge of the immense, sweeping, beneficial effects that this struggle has produced in the moral fibre and stamina of the nations engaged.

It must be remembered that the horrors of the imagination are far worse than the realities. The men who fight and the women who tend their wounds suffer mentally far less than those who paint the pictures in their minds, from data which so very often are grossly exaggerated. One must realize that the hardships of war are merely transient. Men suffer untold discomforts, and yet, when these sufferings are over and mind and body are at ease for a while, they are completely forgotten. The only mark they leave is the disinclination to undergo them again. But on those who do not realize them in their actuality, they cause a far more terrifying effect.

Now, others, as well, have discovered that war's advantages outweigh so much its losses. They who with their own eyes had seen the wonderful fortitude with which men stand pain, and the amazing submission with which women bear sorrow, returned full of zeal and enthusiasm, to carry the torch of this uplifting flame to their own countrymen.

Others will realize, too, that although one may lose one's best, yet one's worst is made better. The women will find that the characters of their men will become softened. The clear-cut essentials of a life of war must make the mind of man direct. It may be brutal in its simplicity, but it is clear and frank. Yet to counteract this, the continual sight of suffering bravely borne, the deep love and humility that the devotion of others unconsciously produces, bring about this charity of feeling, this desire to forgive and this moderation in criticism, which is so marked in those who have passed through the strenuous, searing realities of war. Since the thirty pieces of silver, no minted coin in the world has bought so much as has the King's shilling of today.

Men and Tanks

J. C. MacIntosh

Contents

CHAPTER 1

The Wanderer's Return

Tosh was seated in the officers' coach of a troop-train, waiting for it to start. He had been similarly engaged, off and on, for seventy-five minutes, having arisen with the lark from a comfortable bed at the officers' club in order not to miss what was, according to the local R.T.O., "the only punctual train in France."

As he mused contentedly on his doings of the past fortnight, his eyes roamed over the station platform. Under the watchful scrutiny of two red-caps, a stream of soldiers was entering, reinforcements, if only in virtue of the cleanliness of their iron-ration bags. Between the ticket-office and the hut, sacred to the R.T.O., a glimpse could be caught of that quaint little train by which Tosh had so often journeyed to the seaside health-resort some six miles out of town. As his gaze passed idly along the platform, he noticed two *poilus* clad in faded blue, bedecked, as usual, with the innumerable little haversacks and satchels in which their Army delights.

"On leave, I suppose," he muttered to himself, and thought of the *permissionnaire* he had once encountered, who, from a safe and comfortable base-job, had come on leave to one of the hottest villages behind the line, and had spent a blissful day rooting round in the debris of his paternal mansion.

Suddenly Tosh's eye was caught by a surprising spectacle. Hurrying through the gateway as if his life depended on it, came the most beautifully apparelled of young subalterns. He was hung round about with all manner of map-cases, haversacks, field-glasses, and other "Blighty touches"; from his pink cheeks to his pink breeches, the colour-scheme was a delight to the eye; and he was followed by a diminutive batman, almost obliterated by a most capacious valise. Up dashed the young officer to the coach, perspiringly followed by his faithful, if overloaded henchman. It was then that Tosh noticed the newcomer's badges—the new Tank badge of which he had heard, but which had not yet percolated to France, and on his right sleeve a resplendent tank in black and silver thread.

"Here, Tanks!" he called. "Come in here with me. The other dog-box is for the O.C. train. Send your man with your valise along to the trucks; they're labelled Chevaux 8, so there should be room for it!"

Having taken this advice, the newcomer climbed in and set about divesting himself of his Christmas-tree trappings. On closer scrutiny his appearance somewhat modified Tosh's judgment of extreme inexperience, but that he was essentially a "young officer" admitted of no question.

"So that's the new badge, is it?" remarked Tosh. "Have a gasper? No, they haven't arrived out here yet. Don't think much of them—too much like the A.S.C. and the R.A.M.C., and such-like. You're going up as a reinforcement I suppose—which battalion? So! Well, you're lucky; you've struck the best of the bunch."

Forthwith he plunged into an eulogy of the old X Battalion, which in the earliest days, as X Company, had done such outstanding work, and had continued doing all the best work down to the present time. Such bursts of eloquence are common enough from old hand to new; in the present case it was swallowed eagerly enough. It was explained to the new hand why colours were worn on the; shoulder-strap, and which colours were of good and which of doubtful repute, and why all but the four original battalions were "rainbow" battalions, and many other matters it was good for him to know; and, while Tosh talked, the train bethought it of its duty and hissed and puffed and whistled, and finally crept out of the crowded sidings into the open country.

Tosh surveyed with languid eye the well-remembered scenery. First the huge camp on the hills overlooking the town, row upon row of orderly white tents, with huge parade-grounds—the bull-rings of evil fame; while the other window gave upon flat, marshy little fields set with alders, and behind them, big white sand-dunes with clumps of pine. Soon they were passing through a cemetery, endless little white crosses each marking a carefully-kept grave. Then camps, and again open fields; the train was an express, and did a handsome fifteen miles an hour; and presently they ran beneath the ancient walls of a great feudal stronghold, about whose feet clustered the houses of a modern town.

"G.H.Q.", explained Tosh, "and a very *bon* spot too."

Then out into typical French country, undulating hills, well studded with woods, with the main road running near the line, through many peaceful little villages of white farm-houses and cosy *estaminets*. After an hour's journey, the valley up which they were running gradually widened; lorry-traffic began to thicken on the roads; and they ran easily into a mediaeval town of some size, untouched by the hand of war save for the presence of a few British soldiers.

"H.A.C.", remarked Tosh, "guarding Advanced G.H.Q. They've got some job, I can tell you; they do a week's Cook's Tour in the trenches, and then go back to Blighty for a commission. Oh, you were in Inns of Court, were you? We've got a couple of chaps from there. Were you on guard at the Tower with the Beef-eaters? Rather a good job, too, I should say.

"I? Oh, I've been down at —— for a fortnight, doing a gunnery course. Very comic, I assure you. All the captains in charge were my juniors in the old depot at home, and had never seen any scrapping at all. Still, I had a good time, even if I was threatened with a court-martial for not making notes!"

The train having now made up its mind to tear itself away from the town (which had a place in Tosh's affections by reason of the hot baths to be obtained at the local convent) they ambled along gently to a village a few miles out.

"Here you are," said Tosh, "this is us. Wonder what the billets are like. It's a nice little place—*beaucoup estaminets* and such-like. Hullo, there comes our second in command."

Forthwith he leapt out and strolled off to meet Captain Pilkinson, second in command of his company, a man famous throughout the corps for sound sense and highly-decorative profanity. From him he obtained details as to billets, and went along to the mess for a drink.

"How's life up here, skipper?" he inquired.

"Oh, —— cushy as ——. I've got a lovely billet, with two pukka, high-class girls in it; nothing to do all day; a topping mess, and an officers' club established in the best *estaminet*. The whole battalion's here, without any Tanks, playing round doing arm-drill and semaphore, waiting for something to happen. Here you are; here's the mess—in you go. Hayles, two whiskies! Pretty good, yes, no, hey?"

Tosh, being accustomed to the local idioms, replied that it was pretty good. The mess was situated in the back room of the local school. It boasted two windows (complete with glass), a stove, three tables, easy chairs and the usual tasteful pictures on the walls. Seated round the stove were three officers, with whom Tosh proceeded happily to swap drinks.

"What are you chaps doing?" he asked.

"Nothing at present," replied the reconnaissance officer, "but the air is full of the most disquieting rumours!"

CHAPTER 2

Warning

The rumours of a show in the offing did not develop for several days, and Tosh fell back into the free-and-easy ways of the Tank Corps when incomplete with tanks. He endeavoured to instil into his crew the rudiments of arm-drill, which both he and they had forgotten. He lectured them on visual-training; he let them display their knowledge, and occasionally their ignorance, of the Lewis Gun. And in his spare time, of which there was an astonishing amount, he foregathered with other irresponsibles in the officers' club, drank vast quantities of *café-au-lait*, and, under the watchful eye of Maman Fresnoy-Dubois, flirted pleasantly with Lucy and Jimmie, the daughters of the house.

To this idyllic life a term was set by a sudden announcement in Company Orders:

"The following crews will parade at 8.30 a.m. to take over Tanks as detailed below." Followed a list of crews in which Tosh figured.

Speculation was rife that evening in the absence of the senior officers who were responsible for the order; and, when the workshop officer entered mess, he was immediately greeted with a volley of questions.

"Yes, they're those salved buses brought over from Central Workshops by A Company. The engines have all been "converted"—which means aluminium pistons—and over-heat like blazes; the timing is all wrong; a couple have twisted shafts; and some of them have bullet-holes plugged with putty. However, a little work will do you young lads no end of good. Stand me a beer, somebody."

"That's all very well, Sprockets," replied the reconnaissance officer, usually designated as the R.O. "Because you've been joy-riding round France in a Brigade Sunbeam, and coming late to mess with your hands artistically unclean to produce an impression of work well done—yes, thanks, I'll have a Bass. I suppose you think the rest of the company have been doing nothing. You don't realise how wearing it is, after not touching a hipe for years, to instruct our bright recruitees in arm-drill by numbers. Besides, personally, I've been trying to instil some idea of semaphore signalling into the most thick-headed lot of young officers it's ever been my lot to encounter. Cheerioh, everybody!"

"'Ear, 'ear," applauded Herr Von (so named because of a close resemblance his real name bore to that of a famous Boche air-fighter). "And the price of the pills is twopence per box! I thought myself you'd spent most of your time wrecking other people's motor-bikes. Still, I'll be glad to be shut of all that stuff myself; if we're the Tank Corps we'd better stick to our tanks and get on with the war. Wonder where they'll send us, though-hope to blazes it's not the salient. What do you think, skipper?"

"Not much fear of that," replied Captain Alphen, M.C., commanding 10 Section, who had been enviously reading the "*marraine*" columns in the *Vie Parisienne*. "Ypres is so full of buses stuck in the mud they dare not send any more, or they'd sink it altogether instead of its being only half-submerged. I've heard rumours of a new kind of stunt altogether—a real chance for us at last—to be kept absolutely hush-hush. Anyway, if you take my tip you'll rout out any old equipment lists you can get hold of; there aren't any with the Tanks, and anything that's worth winning A Company will have won by now, I swear."

With which safe prophecy Tosh's section "Well, well," said Herr Von, "come what may, here's luck to our next effort in the Great War"—a toast which was drunk with acclamation.

CHAPTER 3

Taking Over

Next morning the company duly paraded at 8.30, and marched off by sections to the tankodrome, which lay about a mile out of the village along the *route nationale*. The name calls up visions of sandy arenas, where the dust rises high above the whirling wheels as all Rome hangs breathless upon the fate of her favourite charioteer. The reality consisted, *tout simplement*, of a square of churned and trampled mud between green fields. In one corner stood a marquee full of stores, with a sentry striving nobly, and on the whole, successfully, to resemble the soldier he was, and not the chauffeur he had been.

Drawn up in two lines on either flank of the mud-patch, and covered with brown tarpaulins, lay the tanks: "A" and "B" Coy. on the left; "C" Coy.—our company—on the right; 10 Section, with Alphen and Tosh at the head, wheeled off the road into the mud—thereby losing all semblance of military precision-halted, and stood easy, while the tank commanders set about identifying each his own bus, of which he already knew the number.

It may here be explained that a tank possesses two numbers, a manufacturer's number and a battalion number. The former is branded upon its hindquarters at birth, and remains until dissolution; the latter varies from time to time according to which crew are inhabiting the beast at the moment, and is intended to facilitate identification at a distance. As regards names, the choice, alas, is no longer left to the youthful and revue-full fancy of the young tank pilot; names are passed down from tank to tank, and indicate the battalion, and occasionally the company, to which the bus belongs.

"Tank commanders, please march off their crews to take over tanks and check equipment"—thus Captain Alphen.

Let us follow Tosh as he moves his men off.

Their particular "heavily-armoured car," Tank No. 2597, is at the extreme end of the line, and is fully exposed to a cutting cross-wind. Beyond the matter of position and number it has apparently no peculiarities; but Tosh, on whose young shoulders rests a heavy burden of experience, wonders gloomily just what tricks this specimen of devilry will develop on closer acquaintance.

"Overalls on," he orders, and the crew struggle resignedly into "suits combination drill brown," the working dress of the Trade by Land. "Gunners, take off the cover; drivers, bring out all the equipment."

Two drivers, with practised skill, leap on to the rear slope of the track, swing themselves up by the underditching beam (a solid chunk of wood six feet long and one foot square, carried at the stern of the Tank for use in emergencies), and roll up the tarpaulin.

Meanwhile, the first driver, a most important personage, who is responsible for the mechanical efficiency of the tank, proceeds to inspect her interior. "She," curiously enough, is a male, carrying six-pounder as well as machine-guns, and is therefore easy of access. The door is in the rear of the projecting "sponson," or gun-turret, and opens with a key. Having unlocked the door, the arch-devil pokes his head into the gloomy depths, immediately withdrawing it with a resounding curse. The gunners aloft, in rolling up the tarpaulin, have sent a cascade of water down through the periscope-hole in the sponson roof, doubtless as a ceremonial ablution for the new tenant on his first entry. This rite completed, he steps carefully inside.

The inside of a tank is not remarkable for comfort or capaciousness. The centre is occupied by a large engine, the rear by a huge differential, the two sides by field-guns, and the front by seats and driving controls; while the roof is not high enough to allow of standing upright. The fact that eight men frequently spend many crowded hours of glorious life in the remaining crevices does not prevent one man, if careless, from banging his head and both elbows at the same time; especially as the lighting arrangements are artificial and inadequate.

But our friend is an old hand, rendered cautious by many a bump on projecting rivet-heads, and he sets about his business of examination without further ado. Meanwhile, the second driver (understudy to the first, with additional work of his own), and the third driver (cross-talk comedian and general nuisance) enter by the other door, open the tool-boxes in the floor, and throw tools and equipment into a large box outside.

The equipment list of a tank is a document well worthy of study, comprising as it does such a medley of timber, hardware, and iron-mongery as only a salvage-dump could ever rival. As he surveys the welter in gloomy silence, Tosh is reminded of an incident of the very early days when a major, lately transferred from the cavalry, was checking stores. "Wires towing," he read from his list, and was shown twenty feet of wire cable; "wires fuse," and a piece of silver one inch long and one millimetre in diameter was proudly exhibited; "key petrol filler cap" proved to be a large size Zulu *knobkerie* of iron, "key carburettor" being an affair the size of one's little finger.

The major was now hopelessly lost, and when "bars crow one" proved to be a crowbar, his face was wreathed in smiles; but suddenly a horrid doubt crossed his mind, and calling up the subaltern in charge, he whispered, "Look here, for God's sake, don't show me a toothpick and call it 'bars ivory officers for the use of, one'!"

Slowly and methodically Tosh wades through the list of items useful and ornamental, decorative and deadly. Periscopes are there, and plugs sparking; spanners, scrapers, and shovels; gun spares, engine spares, track spares. There is included a fishing net, with green rags tied to it, as a camouflage; there are signalling discs and "flappers" which no tank commander has ever been known to use, but which are still religiously issued and must be exhibited. Gradually order develops out of chaos; the checking is complete, and Tosh writes out a duplicate list of his deficiencies. Meanwhile, the crew stow the various implements away where they fondly hope they will be able to find them in case of need.

The first driver now reports the engine ready to start, "if the —— will start!" Tosh climbs inside and seats himself well forward, out of harm's way, and the three drivers get on to the starting handle. The starting-handle of a tank is no puny touring-car affair; it is supported at both ends, and is so constructed as to give four men a grip. The first driver "trips his mag" and "tickles his carburettor" (operations of tremendous secrecy and importance), the second "engages her," while the third exclaims, "Bejabers, but she'd be hard to start in gear," and proceeds to rectify this omission of the late tenant. Finally all three hurl themselves at the starting-handle, and to a merry click, click, click from the magneto impulse-starter and a thirsty sucking from the carburettor they turn the engine over.

After a minute or two of this exhilarating sport, the engine showing no intention of starting, they stop and mop their brows; then at it again, and so for half an hour they labour and examine and swear and try again. Finally Tosh intervenes.

"Look here, there's only one thing for it—boil some petrol and we'll inject it hot into the cylinders."

The first driver collects a small tin and an old Lewis Gun magazine, both of which he fills with petrol. Repairing to the nearest field, he places the tin in the magazine, and drops a match. The petrol immediately flares up; but, as the flames in the magazine die down, he extinguishes the tin by putting his foot over the mouth, picks it up in a pair of pliers, runs across to the tank, injects the hot petrol with a syringe, and at the fourth turn the engine starts gaily with a splutter and a cough of smoke. This is a device not included in any published manual of *Hints on Easy Starting!*

While the gunners have been inspecting the six-pounders as yet they have drawn no Lewis Guns—Tosh has been examining his seat and the various devices round it. The tank commander's seat, a horsehair cushion, is set well up in the forepeak or cab; as he sits in it, his feet rest on the upward slope where the belly runs up to the curve of the nose. In front, behind, and to the left, are various flaps and "gadgets" for observation; immediately above is a periscope-hole; to the right is a mounting for a Lewis Gun, while beside the commander's seat is that for the driver, with similar flaps and with controls for driving the tank. Tosh tests them methodically, finds them o.k., and climbs outside to look at the tracks.

The tracks of a tank consist of two endless belts running completely round the hull; each comprises some 80 steel plates, linked together flexibly and running in guides. Curiously enough, after a little use the track appears to have stretched and runs quite loose, owing to the bearing surfaces having worn; adjustment is therefore provided, and it is one of the fine arts of tank-driving to keep the tracks evenly and correctly adjusted.

The tracks of Tank 2597 are neither new and stiff nor old and worn; but upon testing them with a crowbar Tosh finds them slack and gives orders to have them tightened. This operation is performed with two huge spanners weighing some five pounds each, and is essentially a two-man job.

This detail having been attended to, Tosh reports himself to his skipper as ready to move off for lunch. The other crews of the section are in the like fortunate condition; they are accordingly marched back to the village and break off for the midday meal.

Thus began a fortnight of strenuous preparation. The tanks a month ago had all been certified ready for action by a body of experts; but the crews which had now taken them over expected shortly to entrust their lives to them, and it was remarkable how much work they found to do on them before they were satisfied. Tosh was more fortunate than some of his friends, who found themselves compelled either to change a twisted shaft or to replace worn sprockets—both highly skilled and difficult operations, entailing much labour, with three-foot crow bars and five pound sledge hammers. He, therefore, in spite of having to draw and test Lewis Guns and load ammunition into magazines, found ample leisure for innumerable adjustments such as his heart delighted in.

Finally came the order to "push in sponsons." This is the immediate and inevitable preliminary to a railway journey, and consists in pushing in the projecting gun-turrets along guide-ways until they are level with the side of the tank. The operation is not a difficult one, but calls for co-operation between tank and tank. All bolts having been withdrawn, one tank noses up to the sponson of her mate and gently but irresistibly pushes it in; the order is then reversed, and the benefactor is rewarded strictly according to his own good deeds. When a tank has both sponsons pushed in, her internal accommodation is scant indeed, and it is with heartfelt relief that her crew crowbar the sponsons out into place again.

In the evening of the day when sponsons had been pushed in, the expected order was promulgated, to wit, that on the morrow all tanks would move to Central Workshops, and there entrain for an unknown destination "up the line."

CHAPTER 4

The First Move

Next morning Tosh rose at an early hour, and watched his batman packing kit. While down the line, the Tank Corp permits itself many luxuries unknown to the "P.B.I," but the wise and experienced do not attempt to carry up the line all the collapsible chairs, beds and baths which have lightened their period of rest. Up the line there is usually material in plenty for ingenious constructions which can be left behind at each move. Tosh therefore made a judicious selection; what was to be left behind was conveyed to the battalion dump, what was to go with him he ordered Jakes to transport in a wheelbarrow (French, Mark 7., "pinched"), to the tankodrome.

At 8.30, being all well and truly fed, the skeleton crews (*i.e.,* three drivers and an N.C.O.) fell in and marched off along the main road. No sooner had they arrived than they were swallowed up in a bewildering whirl of preparation. A company move under these circumstances is always closely allied to a race-meeting; money is invariably placed on the issue, and the competition between crews is something astonishing, for the first arrivals will have first choice of food, billets, and other creature comforts.

Tosh set to work at once packing his stuff. The top of a tank between the tracks is a very narrow space, and the centre is occupied by an unprotected exhaust-pipe which soon becomes red-hot on the move. The difficulty of packing such inflammable material as camouflage nets, valises, and petrol will be apparent. In fact, nothing is more common than the sight of a tank proceeding on its way, the crew inside blissfully unconscious of a furious fire "up aloft "which is destroying the fuel of propulsion, the net of invisibility, and the commander's glad rags in one awful holocaust. Let the crew be warned and immediately, like bees from a hive, they swarm from man-hole and door armed with patent fire-extinguishers which never by any chance extinguish; boxes, tins, valises are flung wide, to splutter in-gloriously in the mud, and while the officer sadly examines the charred remnants of his "posh" field-boots, the crew thank their stars that the ammunition didn't start going off!

The secret of safe packing is in the use of "spuds." Concerning these mysterious articles a word is necessary. They are but distantly allied to the spud which is an agricultural implement; they have nothing whatever in common with the spud which is an edible tuber, but are, in fact, blunt-headed, anchor-shaped steel plates furnished with a central rib, which are clipped upon the tracks of a tank to give a better grip in soft ground. Unfortunately, if the ground is hard (e.g., metalled roads), they are worse than useless, and are therefore carried loose until the time comes to affix them.

Now pack forty of these spuds over the exhaust-pipe and you have, in theory, a fire-proof protection. Nothing apparently could be simpler; but there is a catch somewhere, because whenever and wherever a company of tanks makes a ten-mile move, as sure as death someone will have a fire. Nor would the Tank Corps have it otherwise; in a life of dreary monotony and endless discomfort, why should we abolish anything which tends to provide harmless amusement for the troops?

To return, however, to our muttons. Tosh, having drawn petrol, oil, and grease, and seen it safely bestowed in the bus, having carefully protected his valise and his crew's kits with spuds, being, in fact, ready to move off, turned to listen to a small voice which spoke pleadingly in his ear:

"Please, sir," said the diminutive servant of Tosh's respected section commander, "Captain Alphen says will you take his valise on your tank, sir?"

Tosh had been expecting this. Probably the only point in which the subaltern ever has an advantage over his skipper is that he possesses the beast of burden, while his senior officer does not.

"All right, Jones, I'll take it, provided you get hold of the mess corporal and tell him I have no room to carry his crockery." Satisfied with his bargain, Tosh had the engine started and proceeded to move off.

He was not the first by any means. The unmistakable clatter of tank-tracks filled the air; several quaint shapes were cautiously threading their way through the jumble of the 'drome, while a couple of early starters were already on the road. Tosh was not perturbed. The run would be long and trying; the result dependent more on previous preparation and present good driving than on any spurt off the mark.

One tank commander had already discovered this to his cost. Having neglected to move off very cautiously from a mud-puddle, where his tracks had been stationary for a month, he had snapped the links of a plate, and the broken track, being flexible only in one direction, stuck straight out in front like an ironical signpost. Only half an hour's work, but an unfortunate beginning to a heavy day.

Tank 2597 had better luck and, with Tosh in front directing, safely threaded her way through the tank-lines of the other companies and debouched upon the road. For reasons not unconnected with his comfort, it is an almost invariable rule for the tank commander to walk in front of his tank when she is on the move, the exceptions being first, when the ground is muddy, and second, when the outside air is unhealthy. Tosh, then, is to be pictured strolling leisurely along, hands in pockets, occasionally throwing a glance over his shoulder to see that his faithful beast is following.

It is difficult for those who have not seen one to imagine the extreme slowness and unwieldy deliberation of the original, large, Mark 4 tank. Their maximum speed was six miles an hour.

Almost every change of direction, being accomplished by the slipping out of very refractory gears, necessitated a halt, if only a momentary halt. With care and judgment, however, they could be steered to within an inch, a useful attribute which Tosh had occasion to test.

The direct route to Central Workshops would have been straight along the main road, a distance of perhaps twelve miles; but as the passage of tanks does not improve the metalling of a road, a divergence was made a mile out of the tankodrome, the route running first by country lanes and finally across country, a distance of something in the neighbourhood of twenty miles.

No sooner had Tosh turned off the main road into a very narrow lane, with high banks on both sides, than he met a market-cart completely blocking the way. The horse was evidently unused to leviathans, and snorted wildly; but, being addressed by his driver in the universal gutturals of the farmer, condescended to stand still while Tosh, guiding his crew with uplifted forefinger, steered his craft with such nicety that, while not more than three-quarters of the right-bank was cut away, the paint was hardly brushed from the farmer's cart.

They parted with expressions of mutual goodwill—or so Tosh interpreted the verbal half-bricks hurled at him by the Frenchman. Parisian French is usually considered a mellifluous language; but go to the sturdy peasantry who form the true backbone of France, and you will find their patois as harsh and uncouth as the most earnest philologist could desire.

For some time after this little incident, the journey was uneventful. After a short interval of indecision the road mounted steadily up the right-hand slope of the valley. To right and left, far as the eye could see every inch of ground was under heavy crops, save where a little copse crowned some knoll. As they climbed higher, more and more little villages could be seen smoking peacefully in the blue haze, while right and left ran the straight white tree-lined roads of France. Just so had many another fair valley appeared before it was whelmed in that terror which even now could be heard thundering in the distance.

Tosh felt himself in sympathy with the famous division whose sole motto is "Kill!"

While musing thus, Tosh had the satisfaction of passing the tanks ahead of him by virtue of the superior pulling powers of his engine in third speed. Consequently he was the first to enter the village of Equancourt. As he chuff-chuffed along the main street (the village boasts two streets, the main street and the other one), such of the inhabitants as were not at work in the fields crowded to door and window, with guffaws and schoolboy jests for the lumbering disturber of their peace. This, no doubt, was kindly meant, but Tosh could gladly have got along without it.

Having surveyed the route before, he knew of a ticklish corner ahead where spectators were particularly undesirable. Here the route turned at right angles into a lane just the width of a tank, the jaws of the entrance being the corners of mud houses which would cave in at a touch. The available area of approach was considerably lessened by the presence of the village pond; wherefore the tank must swing at right angles on a flat metalled road.

Now when a tank swings on flat ground, a length of track must scrape over the ground carrying a weight of forty tons. Given soft ground, and the swing can be accomplished in very small space, but on a road it is frequently difficult to swing a tank in less than its own length. By a happy combination of judgment on Tosh's part, and brute force on that of his second driver, the manoeuvre was successfully accomplished; but Tosh learnt later that of the following tanks no less than four brushed the wall of the left-hand house, the last one leaving a gaping hole sufficiently large for the passage of the piano, which could plainly be discerned inside. Result, a furious complaint by the owner, trouble for the tank commander, and a trifling addition to the cost of the war.

Tosh's engine now began to "overheat like stink." As they were approaching a village in which he had been billeted for a month some time before, they carried on until they reached his old abode. Pulling up on the doorstep, Tosh left his crew to shorten the fan-belt, which had stretched after its kind, while he paid a call on his ex-landlady. He was rewarded for his politeness with some excellent coffee, which he shared with the crew; and matters being now shipshape, they carried on. The half-hour halt had put them back to fifth in the race, but within a mile they came to the end of the road part of the journey.

From here on would be downhill, over soft ground; accordingly engines were shut off, and the five crews clambered stiffly through the manhole (the sponson-doors being inaccessible when sponsons are pushed in) and lay down for lunch and an hour's rest.

The crews' heads were humming from the incessant clatter of gear-wheels in a confined space, while the officers had walked ten miles largely with a head over one shoulder. Consequently the hour was not long in passing.

At its conclusion, they started up and set off. Tosh had had enough of walking, so he sat himself on top of the cab in front, leaving the direction to his first driver, but ready, if need be, to signal through the flap.

They were now upon a regular cross-country tank-route—a strip of churned mud thirty yards broad, running between fields green with young crops. In the mud could be seen the spoor of countless Tanks crossing and recrossing. Owing to distribution of weight, it is no deeper in soft mud than a man's; yet on the hardest of roads it will remain for months, the projecting lip of the track being forced in with a forty-ton weight. Only a couple of inches deep on the average, traces of it will remain after months of rain and weather.

The trip now frankly developed into a race. The going qualities of all five buses were much the same; but in matters of steering and tactics there was abundant opportunity for the display of individual skill. What a queer spectacle those crosscountry trips afforded! The group of steel monsters crawling fussily along, tracks clattering, exhausts thrumming, steam pouring out from the radiator-escape in the roof, for all the world as though they are doing fifty instead of five miles an hour. Meanwhile the tank commanders in front, apparently so indifferent, in reality are fiercely eager as to the result, and desperately impatient of the leisurely pace, as they indicate with quick waves where an opportunity shows itself. And at the finish, no spoken comment but how those schoolboy-veterans enjoyed watching the others come in, their own bus the while snugly camouflaged and the crew happy in the nearest Y.M.!

"You know, boys," says Old Bill, "we shall miss this blinking war when it's over." A jest, but with an undertone of truth. How often in the unfriendly atmosphere of later life, we shall look back with longing on the "terrible years," missing their careless, happy-go-lucky *camaraderie*. No need to exhibit the skeleton at those feasts; all had the moral constantly in mind, and the result was a spirit which can never be recaptured save in similar circumstances—which, God in His mercy, forbid!

After a spanking three-hour run, Tosh began to draw near Central Workshops. He had indulged in a small fire—damage, one gasmask, old type, and a corner of the tarpaulin; but was running second. The first sight of their goal came from the top of a hillock, whence they looked down upon the rows of huge sheds, green corrugated iron on steel girders, which comprised the actual shops.

Flanking them could be seen two rows of big hangars—sparepart receiving and distributing shed. In the distance, close to the main line railway which ran up the valley, lay the salvage department, where old hulks reduced, apparently, to scrap-iron, were skilfully built up again into serviceable weapons of war; while above the salvage-shop was the huge square training-ground where new types, new methods, and new devices were constantly put on their trial. Having been concerned six months before in erecting the first hut on this site, which was then empty pasture, Tosh was in a position to appreciate the wonderful growth of this engineer's paradise.

As they ran down the last hill, the tanks passed within a few yards of the barbwire entanglements surrounding the Chinese compound. The placid Celestial was extensively used at Central

Workshops, and under a N.C.O. who understood him was capable of surprisingly skilled work. The "local moon-faces," as the second driver described them, had apparently been celebrating some ancestral rite, for the entrance to their camp was decorated with a splendid arch of red and yellow paper, while Chinese lanterns, whence obtained only their possessors could say, hung on strings between the huts. A few gentlemen of leisure placidly surveyed Tosh as he steamed past; but, to men who could themselves make the puffing devils, it was a matter of small interest.

The route now crossed the road and entered a mud-square immediately above the railway. Tosh ran up beside the first arrival, and filled up with petrol, oil and water from a convenient dump, making a note of the quantities for his daily log sheet, a document rendered nightly by every tank commander complete with tank. Before he had finished Captain Alphen arrived; under his instructions, Tosh marched his men to their billets, saw them comfortable and in hopes of a meal, and trudged happily off to "one of the best messes in France."

This palatial edifice possessed the unusual advantage of being a temporary permanency, and was soundly and cosily constructed. The ante-room boasted an ornamental fire place and a ping-pong table, while round the walls were comfortable cushioned arm chairs. The inevitable Kirchners were set off by water-colour landscapes, while English and French periodicals were strewn carelessly on a corner table. Such are the priceless blessings of a base-job; the combatant officers envied, but did not fume, for they knew the value of the work done and the ready hospitality constantly extended to members of all the battalions.

Talk in mess that evening was animated. Besides the permanent staff, who, as dispensers of new tanks and receivers of old ones, usually had interesting news to impart, there were representatives present of almost every battalion at that time in France. Tosh met many companions of his early training days, and swapped yarns with avidity in the intervals of ping-pong. To crown the evening's enjoyment, the second in command arrived with the glad news that the company was proceeding, not to some sticky part of the line, but to the training-ground on the old Boche trench-system, there to practise a new plan of attack.

"It'll be some place, too, I can tell you—all the battalions are congregating there for three weeks' practice, and then—the real thing!"

On receipt of this welcome intelligence, "C" Company sat down to make a night of it; there was wassail in the great hall till an unchristian hour, and many an officer had difficulty in finding his way to his temporary bed.

Chapter 5

Up the Line

The morning after, Tosh paraded his skeleton crew independently at 8 o'clock and marched off to the tank park. In a few minutes his bus was moving off towards the entraining camp. The route lay between the row of corrugated iron shops and the hangars. Already the shops were busily at work, with a great clanging of hammers and chatter of steam riveters; dirty men in dirty overalls—sergeant-major's last hopes every one of them—were strolling leisurely about with queer tools in their hands, while occasionally a group of Chinese, clad in sky-blue jeans, brimless straw hats, and beaming smiles, were apparently engaged in hindering the passage of *bona fide* workers.

Passing down the corduroy-road, Tosh swung left, taking up a position immediately opposite an inclined timber ramp which finished abruptly in a four-foot drop on to a railway line. These ramps form the regular method of entraining tanks. The specially-constructed tank-trucks are perfectly flat, with very little gap between each, and thus form a long, narrow platform.

The first tank to entrain mounts the inclined ramp and runs directly on to the trucks, passing over them all until it reaches the first; the second tank runs as far as the second truck, and so on. The advantage of being first on the train is, that whereas entraining is usually performed in safety by daylight, when running along a train is a simple matter, detraining is only too often performed under shell-fire at midnight, when it is desirable to have as few trucks to cover as possible.

In the present case, "C" Company's train was not yet in. Entraining was due to start at 10, but before that Tosh had a few spares to draw. Having obtained them from the nearest hangar, he proceeded to inspect his surroundings.

Between the entrainment siding and the main line lay the repair-shop for salved buses. The number of tanks requiring such attention had evidently exceeded expectations; the hangars provided were full, while all the available space in the neighbourhood was strewn with tanks in every variety of disrepair.

A skeleton in the near distance attracted Tosh's attention engine, differential, and radiator had all been lifted out through the roof; both tracks were off and lay extended beside her, while half the nose had apparently been carried away by a shell. Tosh strolled closer—there was something familiar about that nose— and to his surprise discovered her to be one of "C" Company's old buses, half the crew of which he had himself been concerned in burying in a shell-hole near Ypres. Now she was in the hands of six Chinese under a British corporal; Tosh wondered whether, when she was once more fit for service, her new crew would ever hear of her wicked past.

He recognised several others among the many buses, and placed the remainder in their battalions by their names; but soon he grew weary of the incessant hammering of the riveters, and strolled off to the training-ground. Here, parked along three sides of a square, lay the veterans of the corps, old tanks with famous names, obsolete for fighting purposes, but still useful for training and for the testing of new devices. In the square itself were a few of these new devices; among them Tosh noticed one tank carrying on its cab a huge bundle of sticks some four feet high.

Its use appeared problematical, but he distrusted it on principle, little realizing how closely the device would concern him in the near future. In one corner he discovered one of the new "whippets," then still an untried craft, concerning which speculation was rife. He inspected it inside and out with care, and an earnest desire to "see the little beggar go." Close by lay what had

119

all the appearance of a super-tank; in fact, it was a "G.-C," an unsuccessful type subsequently used for supply.

Satisfied with his tour of inspection, he returned to the ramp, where the remainder of the company was now drawn up.

The train was now backed up against the ramp, and "chocked up"—*i.e.*, supports were put up under the ends of the trucks to prevent their tipping up. Tosh started his engine and prepared to move up the ramp.

Entraining a tank is in reality the simplest of operations. But as the train has no raised sides, is barely a foot wider than the tank, and has a habit of swaying as the tank moves along it, the appearance is presented of a most risky proceeding, in which the crew are in imminent danger of an abrupt plunge sideways to the ground four feet below. Further, both the workshops official responsible for the tanks and the R.T.O. responsible for the train are invariably under the impression that the tank commander knows nothing about his job, and is too much of a fool to realize it.

Picture, then, the scene—Tosh in front of tank, which moves slowly up the ramp. To him dashes an excited workshops-wallah:

"Lock your differential now, and come straight ahead."

Tosh takes no notice; he is manoeuvring on the brakes. When the time comes, he signals with uplifted forefinger, and the differential is locked.

"She's not quite straight"—the tab-merchant takes up the tale—"she wants to go a bit right."

Tosh blandly ignores him, signals for a left swing, and stops her; examines her alignment with judicial care—what time the W.O. and the R.T.O. unite in bad advice—approves, and signals her to come on. As she approaches the edge of the ramp, from which there is a slight drop to the truck, the W.O. calls in to the crew:

"Unlock your differential!"

The offender being a major, Tosh contents himself with signalling "washout"—the crew are old hands, and take orders from their commander; Tank 2597 moves gently forward and drops sweetly on to the truck.

"Now unlock," calls Tosh, "and steer on your brakes."

Walking backwards along the train, he watches the edges of the tracks, and as they encroach to right or left upon the few inches of safety, signals the driver for left or right brake. The tank, four feet in air upon a narrow, swaying platform, moves along as safely and as confidently as if on solid earth.

Arrived at the first truck, the tank is "chocked up." To accomplish this, a beam is placed across the truck at a marked spot in advance of the centre. The bus climbs this until her nose is well up in the air. A similar beam having been placed behind her, she is backed down upon this, and is consequently supported quite clear of the truck at two specially strengthened points. With brakes on and engine in gear, she is safe to ride over the most hastily-constructed track.

This operation having been successfully performed, Tosh's crew climbed out through the manhole and began to cover up. At this point the R.T.O. arrived with instructions that the baggage on top must not project more than one foot above the cab. As at present arranged, it projected at least three feet.

"Very good, sir," replied Tosh, and proceeded to shuffle valises and petrol tins.

After considerable labour, the height was reduced to two feet.

"Come on, you fellows, get her covered up quickly and he won't notice; he's back at the ramp now."

The crew drew the tarpaulins over and tied them firmly against the twenty-mile wind they would soon have to withstand, and when the R.T.O. next appeared he passed the bus as fit to travel.

The train was timed to leave in half an hour. The crew made their way to a cattle-truck of the usual type, while Tosh repaired to the little passenger-coach, where his pack had been stowed by his batman. The mess-corporal, invaluable man, had tea on the go, and the officers were sampling the many varieties of chocolate and biscuit they had obtained at the local canteen.

After the lapse of an hour, during which the line had been assiduously watched for signs of an engine to pull the train, the second in command went along to interview the R.T.O. in his cabin half a mile up the line. That superior individual, having been in considerable evidence during the entraining, when his services might have been dispensed with, had now departed for lunch, and would not be back for two hours. A corporal, however, explained the situation.

The engine, it appeared, was expected at any moment, having been delayed by the (French) engine-driver's meeting a friend in the *estaminet* where he ate his breakfast. Unfortunately the day's timetable was made up for this stretch of line, and traffic was heavy and important; consequently the tank train could not have a "march" (apparently the technical term for the right to proceed) before 2.30, when it would be sandwiched between an empty hospital-train and a consignment of heavy howitzers.

For practical purposes, this meant arrival at 3 a.m., and no night's sleep as against arrival at 11 p.m., and a comfortable billet.

"They might have delayed it till to-morrow while they were about it," complained the R.O. "I know a lovely little *estaminet* a mile away, and there's a bioscope in the camp. They never seem to study creature-comforts in this war, do they?"

Further repinings were interrupted by the arrival of lunch. The Tank Corps, having a superfluity of petrol, does most of its cooking by primus stove; consequently, a hot meal can be provided in five minutes under almost any circumstances. What is more, every officer carried in his kit a pocket-primus, over which his servant heats his shaving-water and boils his morning coffee.

The luxurious go so far as to carry toasting attachments, not to make toast, but to warm billets in cold weather, and in winter the genial roar of four "primi" is the inevitable concomitant of an evening bridge-party. A luxurious life, indeed; but there are times when business presses and transport is scarce, when even the Trade by Land must forego its hot-water bottles at night!

At length the dilatory engine arrived, the driver blandly unconscious of the black looks cast at him. He was well aware that there was a war on, but surely it was not every day that the son of his daughter's godfather's cousin came home on *permission*, nor could he, without gross rudeness, refuse to celebrate his return. There is a story of a vital munition train which was delayed for an hour while the driver was hunted for. On being discovered working in his garden he explained that he had observed rain-clouds blowing up, and wished to get his tobacco into shelter before the storm. What a wonderful war it has been, to be sure!

The "march" having at last arrived, the train slowly pulled out of the siding on to the main line.

"Wonder how many of these buses will be back here in two months' time, in the repair shops?" remarked Tosh.

"Cheer up, old bean," responded the R.O. "Look, there's that billet. Damn it, but I'd like to see Jeanne-Marie again!"

The line ran up a smiling valley, studded with little villages. This being the Tank Corps Reserved Area, every village was known to the Company, and concerning every village there was some scandalous story to be told. The sight of a tank-train was here a common event, and the villagers hardly troubled to lift their heads from their work.

"Yes, they are *blasé* enough," remarked someone, "but I wonder how many hours will elapse before the Boche knows all about our having gone up the line! Ah, well, it doesn't matter back here—it's further up we'll have to watch it. Come on, you lumps of cannon-fodder, let's have a game of bridge. All right, poker, then—I always win at poker."

Presently the train ran into the station of a fair-sized town.

"The dirtiest hole in France," grumbled Tosh; "all these picturesque, twisting mediaeval streets, feet deep in filth."

"What about the famous picture-shop?"

"Bores me stiff. Besides, it's too well known to be healthy."

"Yes, that's true," sighed the R.O. "I knew it as a D.R. when the French held it, and it certainly has deteriorated. I know a really nice girl here, though, not the usual *estaminet* type, you know, but a puffick lidy. I met her at Amiens on holiday, but she helps run a little draper's shop here. And anyway, Tosh, we didn't have a bad day here that time we so cleverly missed the train!"

The R.O.'s reminiscences were interrupted by the arrival on the next line of a full Red Cross Train. First came the stretcher-cases, in long specially-constructed coaches; after them the walking wounded, sitting up in the ordinary corridor compartments. Some were yarning, some smoking, some playing bridge, but one and all bore smiles of the most deep-seated cheerfulness. As the train pulled up, from the compartment opposite a man with one arm in a sling, and a Balaclava set rakishly over one ear, called out of the window:

"Hullo, you funny lads, what are you? Pontoon-sections for the Rhine, or Handley-Page Bombers? I shouldn't go in that direction, though, if I were you, there's a hell of a war on up there; people getting hurt almost daily, so I'm told."

"That's all right, my lad," came the response. "Don't get fresh because you pricked yourself on the barbs of the wireless. We're going to win the war, for the sake of brave little Belgium! Don't get engaged to the first V.A.D. who washes your face, will you? You want to pick and choose a bit. My Gawd, don't some people have all the luck!"

The tank train now began to get under way. They parted with many "cheeriohs" and "good lucks"; the one train load bound for what is usually considered the happiest period of a soldier's life; the other for what gentlemen, who doubtless speak with authority, assure us is "worse than hell."

The train now began to enter the fringe of the war zone. Darkness had already fallen, but in all the woods twinkled innumerable lights from the camps of infantry in divisional rest; and Tosh's memory could recall only too well the battered villages and desolate countryside which were now to be his constant surroundings for many a month to come.

The roar of artillery had gradually increased, until the reports of the heavier guns could be distinguished from the muttering of the lighter field-guns, while the horizon was alight with a constant flickering radiance. To the sound of that infernal orchestra, which night and day would accompany their every act and thought, until quiet was become a thing unnatural and to be feared, the officers curled up in corners to sleep as best they might.

Tosh awoke to find the train stationary at a little siding. By that queer instinct which humanity still possesses, in every coach sleepers awoke, conscious somehow that the journey was over. While the train was shunted in against the ramp, crews and officers found their own buses, stripped the tarpaulins, started up cold engines, and ran off the chocking beams. No sooner had the train come to rest than it was "chocked up," and amid the bewildering flashes of the guns the tanks ran off the train.

Tosh, it will be recollected, had driven first on to the train. He was therefore next to the ramp, and left to others the uneasy work of running along the trucks. Once off the ramp, he was instructed by his section commander to "swing right, follow the road to the light railway, cross it, and park for the night." He had been here before, and knew his way, and was soon facing the ramp over the railway. This, the regular type of tank-crossing, consisted in reality of two ramps, one on each side of the line, with space between for the passage of trains.

Tank 2597 nosed carefully up the first; as she came to the point of balance her nose swung down, landing gently but firmly on the second, and she crawled across. One by one the others followed, and drew up in loose formation in the open space beyond. It was then 2.30; at 8 they would proceed on their two-hour crosscountry journey. Without more ado, the crews threw themselves down beside their iron charges, and carried on with the night's sleep.

The light of tomorrow's dawn revealed a picturesque scene. In the lap of a long valley lay what had been at some time a flourishing little village. At the cross-roads still stood the ruined church, while along the village street were the battered remnants of *estaminets* and farmhouses. A broad-gauge railway had recently been constructed through the valley; for station it boasted a row of sandbagged dugouts. By the line of dugouts stood the ramp from which the tanks had been detrained; flanking it the shattered stumps of a few trees, remnants of a large plantation, strove bravely to show green signs of life.

Down the road the tanks themselves loomed out of the mist, queer shapes, in keeping with the unearthly desolation of the scene. A light railway line ran across the valley; following it, the eye was led to the farther ridge, which showed white-tipped; here were the old chalk-cut front line trenches, now used as training ground for H.M. Landships.

Among the tanks there was soon a stir, and a movement. Stiff with cold, and blear-eyed with sleep, the crews set about warming up some breakfast in preparation for their early start. Tosh lifted his head, where he lay between the tracks of his bus, accepted a cup of coffee from his servant, rose, and saluted the sun with a hearty yawn. Before long the beneficent primus stoves had produced hot Maconochie and bacon; the officers settled down near the source of supplies, and dealt with them according to their lights.

"Hell, wasn't it cold!" exclaimed the R.O. "I say, skipper," addressing the second in command, "you don't want me on this fake, do you? The route's as plain as a pikestaff, and most of these lads have been over it before. If I may, I'll stay here and get a decent snack at the *estaminet*; I can always persuade the Yanks to give me a lift on their light railway."

"All right, Uriah Z." replied the second in command, "just as you like. Personally, I'm going over by car. The major will be through at 10—he slept at—last night, and is coming on this morning. There'll be room for you, but not for your kit."

"That's the stuff," responded Uriah.

"Thank God I'm not one of these poor —— who have to look after their heavily-armoured cars. Cheerioh, you chaps, and thanks for the breakfast. I'm going back to bed."

Breakfast over, the crews packed up their kits, and set off along the route. The track from here to the training centre was all cross-country, and countless Tanks had pounded it to a broad flat mud-path. In the first two miles, there was only one possibility of trouble where a broad and unrevetted communication-trench crossed the route. The parapet and parados had been pushed in so as almost to fill the trench; but one of the buses, being carelessly driven, discovered too late that the filling material was soft mud, and buried her nose in several feet of it.

Any attempt to go forward would land her completely in the mud, while her tracks could not grip to pull her out backwards. There was nothing for it but a tow. The following bus hitched on with a tow-rope, stern to stern, and with a steady pull extracted the unfortunate, covered to the eyebrows in liquid mud.

"Well, by ——," ejaculated her disgusted commander, "if you'd told me I *could* have stuck in that ditch, I'd have called you a —— liar."

From here there was for some time but little incident. The route ran in a small depression between cultivated fields; the surface being slippery mud, there was no need to guide the tanks, which no sooner climbed one of the sloping sides of the track than they were automatically returned to the fairway in the hollow. Having nothing better to do, Tosh, who today was inside his bus, pushed up a periscope through the roof and surveyed his surroundings in comfort. As often before, he was smitten with a longing to have a cinema-man film the scene.

There was something at once ludicrous and awe-inspiring in the sight of the antediluvian monstrosities, spouting, steaming and smoking, puffing, snorting and clattering, for all the world like uneasy products of Jurassic slime, as they proceeded with the maximum of noise and bustle at a speed of quite four miles an hour! No wonder the first sight of the tanks reduced the army to the verge of apoplexy. The crews themselves, with every reason for profound melancholy in their knowledge of the "contrary nature of the beast," could not but treat these monsters as a joke until the day when their half-inch of plating was all that stood between them and death!

They were now drawing near their destination. As they breasted a hill, they came in view of a little ruined village in the lap of the valley, where trees which had somehow escaped destruction lined the banks of a muddy stream. On the further slope of the valley was displayed an astonishing spectacle. By sections and by companies, by battalions and by brigades, in quarter column and in mass, lay serried rows of tanks, more tanks than Tosh had seen in his life before, while along the route ahead more tanks were moving to the assembly, and on the near horizon yet more tanks disported themselves on the old trench-system.

Here was no attempt at camouflage, but an open challenge to the Boche: "Tanks? Yes, we have tanks, and we mean to use them. Like to see a few? Certainly," and from all quarters they came, the gathering of the clans of the Trade by Land. Tosh's heart swelled as he looked at them, and filled With speechless emotion.

"Hell! "he ejaculated, and again "Hell!"

The company now began a long down-hill rim into the village. The buses here accomplished fully eight miles an hour, though their tracks clattered as though they would jump the guides. By a dexterous manoeuvre, which very nearly landed him in a 10-ft. ditch, Tosh took second place just before the narrowing road precluded any further attempts at overtaking. Soberly now, and keeping to the right of the road, they filed past the church, round the village green, and up a little road to the Company Park.

The journey now over, the tanks drew up by sections in their appointed place, one of innumerable parks in that teeming zoo. Tarpaulins were stretched over the tracks, and kits unloaded; the crews fell in and were marched off to the tents already erected by an advance party. The officers having selected both tents and tent-fellows, kits were laid out, and Tosh strolled off with Herr Von to inspect the new mess.

The advance party had done their work well. Not only had they acquired a supply of perfectly good duckboards for the camp, but they had seized upon the only house in the village which boasted a roof. True, a 5.9 had punctured the said roof, but a tarpaulin stretched over the hole rendered the place a very home from home. "*Bon*," said Tosh. "*Bon*," agreed Herr Von, and together they drank good luck to the P.M.C. and confusion to his mess-bills.

In company orders that evening appeared a detailed scheme of training for the next week. A certain portion of the trench-system had been allotted to the company. Crews were to parade every morning at 8 a.m., and proceed to the training ground, where they would remain until 3.30, the last hour 3.30 to 4.30 being occupied in filling up for the next day.

Training was to be "intensive," and was designed to give all drivers thorough practice in trench-work (after a long sojourn amid the shell-holes of Ypres) in preparation for a probable offensive. Officers would give all drivers their due share of driving, would insist on strict compliance with service conditions, and would in every case select the most difficult ground available.

With this active life before them, tank commanders were not long in seeking their virtuous couches!

CHAPTER 6

At Play

Next morning, after a hurried breakfast, the crews duly paraded at 8 o'clock, and by 8.15 the tanks were on the move to their playground on the top of the ridge. It may be thought curious that an old and seasoned battalion should require a week's training in driving. The explanation consists partly in the fact that heavy casualties in the salient, particularly among first drivers, had caused some considerable shuffling of duties among the old hands and a drafting in of new details. But, in any case, tank-driving is not the simple business it would appear to be, and constant practice is essential.

The popular idea, largely due to the praiseworthy efforts of sundry newspaper correspondents, is that a tank has merely to be set going, and it will "carry on independent." Should a tree be encountered the tank pushes it over, a house is carelessly thrust on one side, while a trench is not so much as observed by the sublime crustacean.

Alas, how different is the reality! It is true that a tank can push over any ordinary tree (strict orders being invariably issued that trees useful for camouflage must *not* be knocked over); but, should it do so carelessly, the resulting stump will not only ditch it, but may permanently damage its interior. A wall, if it be not too stout, can be demolished; but Heaven help the unwary tank which enters the usual type of house boasting both a cellar and a well! And in the actual crossing of a trench, the daily task of the tank and its *raison d'être*, the most scrupulous care is necessary.

Given good driving and a firm revetment, and our faithful beast will cross almost any trench; but let the driver make the slightest error of alignment, and the bus will heel sideways and be ditched for hours. Let it not be forgotten that a trench in actual practice is not a straight line or even a geometrical figure; it is a bewildering maze of traverse and communication trench, of machine gun and trench mortar emplacements, of dugouts and O-Pips, any one of which is sufficient to engulf a tank for all eternity.

This formidable obstacle does not always boast firmly-revetted sides; more often they consist of crumbling mud, in which the tracks slip instead of gripping. Nor can a jumping place be calmly and carefully chosen from a comfortable coign of vantage; the tank commander and the driver must contrive to choose one amid a hellish crackling of bullets half an inch from their noses, in a shower of red-hot splinters, by squinting through periscopes which are invariably hit and smashed, or by peeping over gun-sights which may admit a bullet at any moment, in face of a well-nigh invisible foe, to whom they are an outstanding target for miles. No wonder, then, that tank-driving is an art, that good first-drivers are rare and cherished possessions, and that "train whenever opportunity offers" is the motto of the corps.

Tosh had been lucky in keeping his old first driver, consequently he devoted most of his attention to his second and third drivers. In common with most of his fellows, he made it a rule never to spend a day without being ditched at least once. "Ditched," it may be explained, is not synonymous with "stuck." A tank which is stuck must be towed or dug out, but a tank which is ditched can usually be extracted under its own power by use of unditching gear. This consists of a 100-lb. beam of wood which can be hitched on to the tracks, and passing under the belly will pull the bus out of many an awkward place. The attaching of the beam necessitates two men climbing out of the bus, but, owing to the protection afforded by her stern, the operation can be, and frequently has been, performed under fire.

Day now followed day without much to differentiate them. In the morning, Tank 2597 would sally forth bright and early, crossing first a railway ramp, then a thirty-foot deep ravine lined with dugouts, an obstacle whose width rendered it easy of passage, the slope being hardly more than 1 in 1. Next she would encounter in succession the reserve, support, and front-line of the British system. Into these she would scarcely dip her nose; for here, as ever, the British dug lightly, while the Boche dug deep. It was after crossing no man's land that she would meet her troubles.

The trenches here were cut in chalk, and frequently went down twenty feet, while from parapet to parados they measured at least twelve. Having chosen his spot with the utmost care, the driver would bring her nose gently forward over the trench till he felt her begin to swing; then throwing out his clutch, ease her down until with a crunch she landed on the opposite wall, her deck at a slope of thirty degrees, and the view from the front flaps "mud—pure mud." Then, letting in his clutch, he would bring her gently up till a thud told him that her tail was on the fire-step.

Then would come the crucial moments. Craning his neck to peer through the flap, which then gave on nothing but blue sky, he would throttle well up; for a palpitating second or two she would hang undecided 'twixt sky and earth, her deck at 50 degrees and her crew hanging on by tooth and claw; then, with an easy motion, she would swing over the crest, the driver at first sight of earth easing her until with a gentle thump she landed again on an even keel.

So much for the ideal crossing. But, as has been mentioned, nothing varies more in width and slope than a trench; all sorts of complications are introduced by dugouts and emplacements; and Tosh invariably succeeded in getting ditched once a day by attempting possible, but not probable, crossings.

On one occasion, when he was making for no man's land in order to stop for lunch, he approached a wide, but fairly shallow trench, with a deep gaping dugout to the left. He did not trouble to swing, judging that he would safely miss; but unfortunately the ground over the mouth of the dugout was soft. As the Tank crossed, it gradually heeled over, while the left track, as it went round, tore away more and more of the indispensable margin of safety.

Muttering, "Don't go down the mine, daddy," Tosh stopped, and got out to consider the position. Useless to try the unditching beam; a drop into that cavern might well be a permanent halt; nothing for it but a tow. Accordingly he dispatched a man to fetch the nearest tank.

Meanwhile a dear old white-haired gentleman had made an unobserved approach. He wore on his shoulders crossed swords, whereat Tosh saluted; he wore on his face a friendly smile, whereat Tosh said, "Good morning, sir," Forthwith they fell into friendly converse one with the other. The brigadier, it appeared, was chief claims officer for the area. He had never seen a tank before, and noticing one from the road had left his car and came across to see it. He showed the most flattering interest in all Tosh had to say; and, on the approach of Herr Von's tank to give a tow, chuckled with pure delight as, with a heave, she pulled her unfortunate friend out of her awkward situation.

"The most interesting thing I've ever seen," declared the brigadier. "I wouldn't have missed it for anything. Thank you so much!" and he departed as pleased as a child.

"As though I'd —— well ditched myself for him to see me pulled out," commented Tosh to Herr Von as they munched army biscuits and cheese. "Still, I love entertaining the old dears and, thanks to you, there's no harm done. But, blazes, supposing I had gone down into that blasted pit!"

For all his love of adventure, Tosh did not actually go down any "blasted pit"; and it was left to another number of the company to perform the finest ditching feat in its history.

At one point in the line there was a triangle of trench enclosing a pond. The gentleman in question crossed the base of the triangle, and was then faced with a difficult problem in tank-tactics. If he reversed, his chances of getting across the trench were very problematical; if he went forward, everything depended on the depth of the pond. He was unwise enough to prefer the hidden danger.

With a merry squelching his tank put her nose down and crawled forward. Every foot forward seemed to mean a foot deeper into liquid mud, until finally the water began to bubble through the holes in her flooring.

At this point, violent efforts were made to reverse, but it was too late; the rising tide had reached the carburettor, and with a gasp the engine died. Even this achievement did not satisfy the envious flood; gradually it rose until the crew, fearful of drowning like rats in a trap, crawled through the manhole in the roof, and stood, a piteous sight, shipwrecked amid a sea of mud.

Unluckily for the commander, he had strayed to an unfrequented part of the course. In the fast-failing evening light never a sail could he spy across all the leagues of mud. With a sigh he made up his mind. Leaving one man to stay with the ship, he gathered his crew together, and one by one they leapt from the friendly platform, waist-deep into ooze, and waded to shore.

Half an hour later a shamefaced young officer reported his plight to the second in command. "Damn it, man," was his comment, "you ought to be in the Inland Water Transport!"

As the story went round, inextinguishable laughter arose from all the tents (officers for the use of) of the host, and excursion parties were immediately organized: "Sixpence to row round the stranded tank by moonlight."

The major, however, saw little occasion for mirth in the situation. He was proud of being in command of the best company of the best battalion in the corps, and he foresaw endless chaffing if the story once got about. Further, he considered this a splendid opportunity for exhibiting that cast-iron discipline for which he would fain be famous. Accordingly, he applied the standing order that crews of ditched tanks will in all cases remain with their tank until ordered to abandon it, thus dooming our friend to a cheerless night in some dugout in the old Boche line.

A special order was issued to all ranks forbidding mention

of the occurrence, while, early next morning, two tanks sallied forth, and, pulling in tandem, dragged the unfortunate from its inglorious position.

Shortly after, volunteers were asked for to man a new type of tank—desiderata, intrepidity and experience. The first to be recommended by the major was the hero of the episode of the subaqueous tank.

In such strenuous but amusing fashion a week quickly slipped by. At its close mysterious rumours began to circulate, in the way rumours have, concerning a new unditching device. Details gradually began to be heard. Others besides Tosh had observed the huge bundle of sticks carried on a tank at Central Workshops; this, it was stated, was the new "Tank fascine," to be carried on the cab of the tank and dropped into any trench or water which appeared too deep to cross.

"C" Company were unanimous in describing this idea as piffle. In their experience it was not the depth of a trench, but the depth of the mud in the bottom or the softness of the walls which caused tanks to stick; and neither of these difficulties could very well be foreseen. Besides, a colossal bundle of wood, if securely fixed, would take a good deal of dropping, whereas, if it was insecurely fixed, it would fall off at the first bump. And to go to so much trouble for a device which could only be used once appeared ridiculous.

Notwithstanding this unanimity, the rumour persisted. It was now stated that a fascine was already on show at the Driving School two miles off, and that shortly they would be issued to all tanks. The matter had now definitely passed beyond the realm of pure fancy; consequently no one was surprised, though many were pained, when a supplement to company orders gave full details of the New Tank Fascine.

The fascine, it appeared, was composed of seventy-two ordinary road-fascines bound together by chains, the resulting bundle weighing one and a half tons. Its inception was due to the habit the Boche had lately developed of digging his trenches very wide, probably as tank-traps; for it was thought that a load of one and a half tons of wood, standing four feet high, dropped even in the ugliest trench, would go far to render it practicable.

The fascine was provided with two chains, by means of which it could be hitched on to the tracks and pulled up on to the cab. In travelling it was to be carried securely fastened; but, before action, would be tilted forward until nothing but an iron hook one inch thick held it from falling. At the psychological moment, a lever inside would release the hook, and the fascine would drop neatly into the trench. A demonstration would be given next day by the brigade fascine officer.

Loud and long raged the argument in mess that night. One man was obsessed with the awful prospect before tank commanders of leading tanks into action in the dark with one and a half tons impending over them, and only prevented from falling on their devoted heads by a movable hook one inch thick.

"Damn it all," he remarked with heat, "we'll have to put barbed wire on the lever, or they'll squash us flat when they think they're locking the diff."

"Yes," agreed another, "and it's not as though we didn't cause enough trouble already pulling down overhead signal-cables, without having four feet of superstructure to help with the good work. Besides, how the hell are we to travel with them? The railway people won't allow a four-foot bundle on top of our buses; we'd wreck every bridge and signal in the place."

"Aha!" cried the R.O., "I have special information on that point. It will all be explained to you tomorrow. You drop your fascine on the truck in front of you before you start, and pick it up again before detraining."

"My Gawd," commented Tosh, "a nice job at two *ak emma* on a cold morning, with no lights allowed and a six-hour drive ahead of you! I'll have something to say to that brigade fascinator!"

A shout of laughter greeted the new title, and word was quickly passed that Tosh had made another of his jokes. Ordinarily a somewhat morose individual, he was given to unexpected flashes of wit. This particular *bon mot* was felt to supply a need, and in a day or two the very brigadiers were to be heard asking petulantly for "my fascinator."

The name gained added point at the demonstration next day. The fascinator proved to be a finicky little man with glasses, who bore all the marks of an ex-schoolmaster. When the officers and first drivers of the Battalion had gathered round him, he opened the proceedings with a lengthy, if eloquent, description of the trials and difficulties experienced by the early tank crews in negotiating trenches. These remarks would no doubt have produced a greater impression on an audience not composed almost entirely of those early crews.

Passing deftly to present conditions, he mentioned that, from intelligence received, the Boche was now digging his trenches even wider, as a precaution against tanks, and explained that in consequence a certain major had devised a fascine to be carried on the tank to assist in crossing these super-trenches. He then described, carefully and minutely, the construction and use of the fascine.

His audience had already absorbed this information from company orders, and were by now thoroughly chilled by the evening breeze. Consequently it is to be feared that, when the fascinator proceeded to practical blandishments, he did not receive that polite attention he doubtless merited. In fact, being unused to command, and exceedingly unused to the command of a tank, he became so involved in orders and counter-orders to the men outside, coupled with signals and counter-signals to the drivers inside, that it was a full half-hour before, amid subdued but derisive cheers, the huge fascine was majestically lifted into the air and deposited upon the cab of the tank.

But this was far from being the end of the show. The written instructions laid it down, that great care must be taken to ensure

(1) that the fascine rested on the flat portion specially provided for that purpose, and

(2) that the fascine was accurately centred with the tank. The

demonstrator was not the man to disobey the letter of the law. Under his orders, two men climbed upon the back of the tank and, with short baulks of timber, propped between the fascine and the track, which was rotated back or forward as might be desired, for a full half-hour they manoeuvred the bundle up and down on its uneasy perch, until at length, amid the apathetic indifference of the instructed, the instructor declared himself satisfied.

As a grand finale, the fascine was eased forward into the "fighting position"; the driver inside touched the lever and, with a terrific bump, the fascine fell to the ground.

"Well, by ——," was Tosh's comment, "if we've got to go through that job entraining and detraining, in the dark, on top of an open truck, and then go forward with that bundle of firewood tilting over threatening to drop on us at every bump, all I can say is, Gawd help the poor tank commander!"

Chapter 7

Rehearsals

Next day the major called his officers together, and lifted slightly the veil of secrecy which so far had obscured their future doings. An attack was shortly to be made on a certain sector; an attack in which tanks would play a very important part. Extreme secrecy was essential to success; given that secrecy success of an unusual brilliance was, humanly speaking, inevitable (we do not quote the major's own words, which were more after this fashion: "Damme, keep your mouths shut and it's an absolute sitter.") That very afternoon would be held the first of two practice attacks with the infantry who would co-operate with them in the real thing.

Now that the subject was no longer taboo, there was a lot of excited speculation as to where the attack would be made, and what it portended. That it was no minor show was clear from the number of battalions who would take part, also from the name of the division with whom "C" Company was to co-operate. The prospect of an attack is not invariably a cause for congratulation, but, in this case, the battalion had so long been out of action, and their last show had been so full of difficulties and disappointments, that officers and men alike were delighted at the prospect of "getting Jerry on the hop."

At two o'clock that afternoon "C" Company set forth in line ahead to the rendezvous, some two miles off. At the first jump they encountered a company from another battalion, bound in the same direction, and there ensued some slight bickering at the cross-roads. The other company were being escorted by their colonel in person, and he saw fit to uplift a stentorian voice in reproof of "C" Company blocking his way.

Now it is a remarkable property of a tank that, whereas all orders delivered from outside to the crew inside, no matter how they are shouted, are almost inaudible, the slightest whisper of the crew inside is as audible outside as if it had been shouted through a megaphone. Tosh had often reminded his crew of this fact, and reproved them for undue expressions of their opinions concerning his orders, but, on the present occasion he rejoiced exceedingly to hear a foghorn voice exclaim, "Damn the silly old ——, does he think his bunch have bought the place? Why, we'd squashed our hundredth pill-box before his young lads had finished buying their rainbows at Harrods."

The colonel half-turned, and for an awful moment Tosh awaited the outburst, but none came, and they proceeded unreproved on their way.

Soon they arrived at the jumping-off point, and drew up in line facing four rows of flags which distinguished respectively the first, second, third and final objectives. The infantry having arrived, the crews of the tanks actively fraternised with their platoons what time the officers synchronised their watches. The infantry then retired 200 yards behind the tanks, the crews climbed in, and machine-guns were thrust through the mountings.

Precisely at zero, the line of tanks moved majestically forward, crushing great swathes of wire, and advanced to the first objective. At their signal, the infantry doubled up and occupied the trench, whereupon the tanks proceeded to the next objective. To a spectator, the scene may have been realistic and impressive; to the participants it was too tame to be even amusing. The last objective having been successfully assailed, the infantry fell in and marched off, while the tanks wandered off to amuse themselves a little before coming home to roost.

That evening, to their intense surprise, "C" Company were informed that their practice, elementary as it had been, had indicated to the staff several weak points in their plans. These would be rectified, and secret instructions might shortly be expected. Meanwhile, "carry on as before."

The company, however, had become rather tired of wandering aimlessly over ground of which they already knew every inch. Accordingly, a plan was made to hold a race meeting, with a prize of five *francs* to the first crew home, and another of ten *francs* to the driver who gained most points for style.

The course was duly set with flags at an early hour next morning. By special arrangement, a portion of the line belonging to another company had been borrowed for the occasion; besides being unknown to the drivers, this had the additional advantage of having been heavily shelled. Beginning in no man's land, the course crossed five particularly nasty trenches in quick succession, space being allowed at the jumps for two tanks only at a time. It then described a half-circle on a steep slope, and returned by the way it had come. Finally, each tank had to describe a figure of eight without making a stop.

Ten minutes before the start, all crews are hard at work getting their charges into fighting trim. One commander can be seen running slowly backwards and forwards, oiling his tracks; another is greasing his gears; a third drying his brake bands, and so forth. Finally, all line up at the starting-point; the starter drops his flag, and they are off.

The first anxiety, as may be imagined, is to be first at the gap. This is largely a matter of starting in a straight line for it, every subsequent adjustment of direction entailing a loss of speed. Imagine a youthful veteran, frantic with eagerness, shut up in a sardine-tin, which cannot be forced to travel faster than five miles an hour, and you will have a fairly accurate picture of Tosh. Here, when there is no opportunity of manoeuvre, he can hardly sit his seat he is so impatient.

Gradually the throng begins to separate out, Tosh running third; the tanks run up to the first jump, change gear, and slowly put their noses into the trench. No racing here, for a judge observes every movement, and every bump means a mark off the total for the higher prize. Tosh's driver, by a masterly gear-change, pulls up level with the second tank. Neck and neck the two amphibians dip their noses, climb slowly to an angle of forty-five, swing gently down again into the second dip (for this is a hog-back), climb again, settle on an even keel, change gears, and dash off again after the leader.

The ground here has been shelled, and the tanks are never for an instant on level keels. Dipping, lifting, slithering, bumping, they race to the second gap and cross it. The next jump is a communication trench at an angle to the first two and to the right. Tosh, being on the left, the necessary swing throws him back to third again, and until the homeward journey begins he has no opportunity of pulling up.

At the last jump of the outward stretch, which is also the first jump of the home stretch, some ten tanks are jumbled together at the gap. When it is remembered that a tank does not turn and advance at the same time, but swings bodily in changing direction, and that no one driver can see any of his opponents' faces, it can be imagined what a riot of confusion reigns as the two streams meet, and what a picture these queer craft present to the perplexed judges, the leaders dipping and climbing successively at all angles with the sky, while those in the rear swing restlessly right and left in a vain endeavour to find a space.

Very quickly the tangle sorts itself, showing the original leader well ahead, next two tanks almost level, of whom Tosh is slightly ahead, and after them a string who hope to gain by good driving what they have inevitably lost as regards speed. At the next jump Tosh, according to usual practice, changes down to second speed. But his rival, noticing that the parapet has been considerably flattened by the passage of so many steam rollers, dashes gaily on in third, dips his nose, meets the trench wall with a bang, climbs laboriously out, picks up speed and is off, leaving Tosh gaping.

But all is not over between them. Taking a leaf out of his enemy's book, Tosh attacks the shelled ground, not in third, in which it can be easily taken, but in fourth. Now a tank in fourth has no climbing power; accordingly all shell-holes must be rushed. Luckily the ground is soft, but, even so, the jolts and jars endured by the crew of Tank 2597 are enough to dislocate their collar-bones. Not for nothing are they endured. At the final jump Tosh is again level, and, in virtue of his drivers' skill in quick gear-changing, runs second past the post.

The final test, a figure of eight without a stop, is more difficult than it appears, for reasons not unconnected with the type of bus in use at the time; but it is smoothly and successfully accomplished. Tosh then draws up at the starting-point, and stops his engine. The crew tumble out, and proceed to chip the winners on their "blinking aeryoplane," while they watch the belated arrival of the "also rans."

The judges now meet to decide upon their award. The first prize presents no difficulty and has been won by the driver usually cited as the best in the battalion. The second and larger prize, however, for good driving, is not so easily awarded.

The first tank in, it appears, did not succeed in completing the figure of eight without a stop. Of the next two, there is some divergence of opinion as to whether Tosh or his rival was more correct in his manner of taking the C.-T. jump. Tosh, it will be remembered, took it slowly and smoothly; his rival took it bumpily but fast. Finally, it is decided to divide the prize between the two; Tosh's driver therefore receives five *francs*, and immediate plans are made for a celebration in the nearest *estaminet*.

Next day, at lunch, typed sheets, marked "Secret," were distributed to all the officers. They proved to be detailed orders explaining the new method of attack, both from the tank and from the infantry point of view. The officers immediately set to work to get them by heart, discussing together all doubtful points and obtaining explanation where necessary.

The instructions dealt with co-operation with the infantry, and fixed a code of signals; they also gave definite and stringent directions concerning the use of fascines. Finally, the major announced that next day the revised plan would be practised in full detail, except for the use of actual fascines; while after the practice twenty of the infantry officers would be entertained in mess. The R.O.'s comment being "Hell! Some blind!"

Next morning, after a short, explanatory address to the men, the tanks moved off to their rendezvous, passing on their way the field-kitchens of the brigade they were to work with. Punctually, as they took their allotted places, the infantry deployed behind them; watches were checked, and all was ready.

The ground had been chosen with great care, so that the obstacles to be met with in the actual attack were represented in the practice at approximately the correct distances. The wire, too, had been untouched by salvage parties; consequently the infantry, in order to pass it, must follow out their detailed instructions.

Zero came, and the tanks moved forward across no man's land. From beginning to end everything went without a hitch. Direction was kept, distance was maintained, the new and complicated fascine-evolutions were correctly performed. Three hours of steady work saw the infantry cold, while the tank crews were hot, but all alike were confident of success as soon as their chance was given them.

Down at the mess that evening the officers, arrayed for the nonce in slacks and shoes instead of breeches and gum-boots, were awaiting their guests. The invitation had been issued from major to colonels with the idea that fraternization would thereby be assisted and good feeling between the co-operating arms be ensured. The mess-president, as a further step towards ensuring this good feeling and co-operation, had obtained from canteens far and wide a two-ton lorry load of Scottish milk.

At five minutes to seven the Jocks arrived, and an appetiser was partaken of. The two parties then sorted themselves out into groups according to the part each was to take in the coming attack, with the result that when they sat down to dinner each tank commander was next to the platoon commander who would be following him into action in a few days time.

The circumstances, and the whisky, were propitious; fraternization proceeded at an unprecedented rate; and co-operation was so far ensured that in a short time many a platoon commander had his arm round the neck of his mate of the tanks, while together they made completely successful attacks on bottle after bottle of "the creature."

Were we living in a freer and less decorous age, when it was the part of a gentleman to require assistance to his couch, it might be recorded that, though the colonels and majors retired at eleven, wassail continued in the great hall till two next morning; that the visitors were carried one by one to their lorry and dumped in it without a groan of protest; while the hosts staggered shouting and singing to bed, each under the guidance of two lusty batmen. As it is, the simple statement will suffice, that parade next morning was called, not at eight, but at eleven, and that before that hour there was much brewing of coffee in officers' tents.

CHAPTER 8

Moving Up

The battalion was now complete, and co-operation with the infantry had been practised. Consequently, it was not long before orders were received to entrain for some destination unknown.

From this time forward every move must be made at night, and every precaution taken to preserve secrecy; but, as the journey to railhead was on a constantly used route, the company set off at two o'clock one afternoon. Sponsons, by a special dispensation, were to be left out.

As usual, the tanks were loaded skyhigh with all manner of merchandise. As usual, the proceedings took the form of a race-meeting. The particular incentive this time was first choice of the fascines which were to be picked up before entraining.

The matter of picking up a fascine had all the appearance of a simple business. But when Tosh arrived to inspect the goods, he was confronted with a confused bunch of bundles of wood, all liberally encrusted with thick mud, and all apparently in that state of shapeless decay against which the fascinator had specifically warned him. Making his choice from among these dilapidated wrecks, he brought his tank up, nose on, and scraped away the mud to find the necessary links.

After some five minutes of this unpleasant work, he discovered the links to be underneath the fascine. His faithful bus was not long in rolling the bundle over; Tosh then found he was on the wrong side. Meanwhile another bus had come up to a fascine close by and completely blocked the way round. Tosh gave his monster a bun and told it to be quiet for a few minutes.

The obstructing tank, having finished its part of the performance, gracefully backed out of the way; Tosh got busy, and in a short tune his ton of sticks was secured weirdly, but adequately, up aloft. The crew then broke off, and Tosh repaired to the local *estaminet* for an omelette and *pommes de terre frites*.

"C" Company's train was due to arrive at 9 o'clock. By 8.45 the tanks were stretched in two lines along the road, ready to entrain by the two ramps simultaneously. By 10 an R.T.O. had arrived to issue instructions for what had already been done. By 10.30 the tram had arrived, and by 10.45 the business of entraining had definitely begun.

Entraining at night when lights are allowed is a simple matter. The tank commander keeps his torch directed on one track. According as the space between the track and the edge of the truck increases or diminishes beyond the correct nine inches, so does he signal with his torch for left or right brake. None the less, the succession of weird shapes, flickeringly illuminated by torchlight and gun-flashes as they crunch their way along a narrow platform four feet in air, form a sufficiently picturesque spectacle.

The local R.T.O., being apparently new to the job, must have thought it dangerous as well, and made himself particularly objectionable; but a few perfectly audible whispered comments by Tosh's crew soon put him to flight, and Tosh found his truck without difficulty.

The real business of the evening then began—dropping the fascines on to the trucks in front of the tanks. From the amount of breathless profanity which rose into the night from up and down the train, it might have been judged that hopeless and helpless confusion reigned; but this would not have been a true deduction, for within half an hour every tank had gently deposited its burden in front of it, and was chocked up securely for the journey.

Up to this point there had been no faintest indication, though there had been many guesses, as to the company's destination. But when the officers had collected in their carriage, word went round that tonight they would only do half the journey, lying up next day in a wood; tomorrow night they would go by train to railhead and then drive some eight miles to another wood a mile behind the front line. "And from there," explained the second in command, "we poop off into the blue."

Meanwhile the train had got under way. It appeared that for two nights this portion of the railway system had been entirely reserved for tanks; accordingly there were none of the usual interminable halts at intermediate stations; and, the train having been "whacked up" to a useful twenty miles an hour, they arrived at their detraining point at three *ak emma*, the chilliest hour of a chilly morning. A thick ground mist had arisen, making it intensely dark; and an order had been issued that lights must be shown as little as possible. It was with no particular joy that the crews turned out to their cheerless task.

Cheerless indeed it proved to be. The chains of the fascines were clammy and intensely cold. The crews fumbled desperately with bolts and nuts, sucking their frozen, muddy fingers, and cursing breathlessly in the peopled dark. Engines were difficult to start, gears were stiff, chocks were jammed—everything conspired to make a difficult task more difficult. And, when the fascines were at last lifted and secured, there was still the slow and laborious work of detraining without lights.

However, all evils have an end. A time came when the last tank had lumbered off the train, slithered across the half-mile of mud, and nosed its way carefully into the luxuriant and thorny undergrowth of the little wood. Camouflage nets were drawn over the tanks; bivvies were constructed of spare tarpaulins, and the weary crews dropped off to sleep.

Tosh was awakened earlier than he could have wished by an all-pervading chill. Seeing no prospect of breakfast for some time, he rose and viewed the countryside.

The wood into which they had driven the night before was now full of tanks, which had crushed ways in all directions through the undergrowth. Walking down one of these ways, and leaping such occasional trenches and dugouts as it crossed, he arrived at the edge of the wood and proceeded to take his bearings.

Across his front ran the railway by which they had arrived, the detraining ramp showing clearly away to the left. Immediately beyond the line, and parallel with it, ran a straight road, while through the trees lining it it could be seen that the ground fell sharply to an invisible valley.

Tosh strolled across the line. As he approached the road, he was struck by a certain familiarity in the general aspect of the country. Now French country, whether strafed or unstrafed, is apt to repeat itself. If strafed, the features are mud and mangled trees; if unstrafed, there is invariably a wood and a straight tree-lined road. Tosh was well aware of this peculiarity, and it was not till he was fairly on the road and looking across the valley, that all doubts were removed, as he recognised the very trench in which for a month he had lived so uncomfortably.

Since those earlier days there had been attacks and retreats; the front-line was now some fifteen miles away. As Tosh thought of the good friends who were with him in that trench, whom he would never see again, he had a foretaste of the mixed feelings with which, "*après la guerre*," we shall revisit our ancient battlefields.

The sun being now well above the horizon, Tosh returned to find breakfast awaiting him.

"Hullo, you chaps," he greeted his fellow-officers, "do you know where we've got to? We're only about six miles south-east of ——. Pity we'll be busy today; there's a *bon estaminet* over there."

"Damn good job you will be busy," replied Herr Von, "'you'd be getting into mischief, and enjoying yourself as if there wasn't a war on."

Busy the crews undoubtedly were that day. It was their last chance of free movement by day, and any further time for preparation was likely to be short. Furthermore, fascines were to be carried in position during the final move, and must now be adjusted so as to require the minimum of attention before action.

It was not till five that crews were dismissed, with orders to be ready to entrain again at ten.

At ten the company moved out of the wood, and took up a strategic position opposite the ramp, which was for the nonce entirely innocent of tank trucks. The night was clear and bitterly cold, with a north-east wind. The crews had had about six hours sleep out of the last forty-eight, and were consequently in the right state of mind to enjoy the hours of hanging about which seemed to be before them.

News soon circulated of an accident along the line, which would delay their entraining for two hours. On receipt of this cheering information, the crews gathered together to have company in their misery. Then some individual, one of our nameless heroes, had a heaven-sent inspiration. The countryside was littered with empty petrol-boxes. At his suggestion these were collected in the dip of a sunken road, a light was put to them, and in five minutes the entire company was dozing contentedly round a flaming bonfire, which, as Tosh sleepily murmured, was indeed *bon*.

True, faces were scorched while backs were freezing, and there was not seating accommodation for all; but on such a night 'twas bliss to be even sectionally warm, and there is a stage of weariness at which standing ceases to be an effort. In fact, it was with profound regret that the company heard of the arrival of their train at 12.45 a.m., and, abandoning the glowing coals of the fire, started up their engines and drove on to the train.

A curious fact was now revealed. It appeared that the whole Tank Corps in France was on the move that night, while there were only a limited number of special tank trucks. The older and more experienced battalions, therefore, were to travel on ordinary heavy-gun trucks; and with a mixture of annoyance and amusement the veterans recognised those queer, humped trucks on which the first tanks were conveyed.

At each end of these trucks was a beam, which each tank must jump, and, as there was quite a wide gap between successive trucks, the chances of the tank side-slipping over the edge were not as minute as one could have wished.

As ever with the Trade by Land, care was the secret; and before long all buses were safely entrained. The crews sent up a pious thanksgiving that for this journey sponsons might be left out, and fascines be carried on the cab. Further, tarpaulins need not be unrolled, crews would travel with their tanks, and engines might, if so desired, be kept running. These indications of a short trip were not belied, and within two hours the train halted, and after some shunting the trucks were run up against a detraining ramp.

Orders had been issued forbidding lights; and, from what they had been told, the officers knew that they were not far from the line. But, if so, it was an unusually quiet part of the line. The silence was profound, and was only occasionally broken by the distant boom of a gun. They welcomed the change from the scene of their last show, where railhead was constantly bombed and shelled, where the sky was alight with gun-flashes and the air heavy with never-ceasing thunder.

Amid this unearthly silence, the tanks crept carefully off the train on to a metalled road. Tank commanders then received orders to collect at the ramp. Here they found the major, who had arrived by car. He explained that they were five miles from the line, and would be in view of the enemy most of the way forward; nor must they suppose that because he was silent he was not watchful. There lay before them a nine-mile run; the time was then 3.30, and they must be in the wood before day broke at seven. The going being mostly flat grass-land, they must make all possible speed.

The subsequent run will always live in Tosh's memory as one of the longest three hours he ever spent. After a preliminary half-mile of road came a three-mile stretch of absolutely featureless country. The sole visible landmark was the broad white tape marking their route; the sole variety an occasional star-shell in the distance. Walk he must in case of hidden pitfalls, but to a dog-tired man the monotony was almost insupportable.

Eventually they emerged again upon a road, and followed

it for dreary miles. It was lined with trees which had not been trimmed for years; their branches almost met overhead, and Tosh had to be constantly on the watch lest his fascines be swept off the cab.

For an area where an offensive was brewing the roads were marvellously empty; but on this stretch they did pass a few limbers. The night was still too dark for clear seeing, but, as the east began slowly, and it seemed unwillingly, to lighten, Tosh noticed by the roadside carefully camouflaged gun-pits (as yet empty of guns) and covered stacks of ammunition. He was subsequently to discover that the whole country was "stiff" with gun-pits similarly empty, which never held a gun until a few hours before the fateful dawn of the offensive.

They had now been two hours on the run, and only an hour of safe movement remained. Already the dawn was breaking, and Captain Alphen told Tosh that they were still a long way from home. But with the dawn came the solution of the difficulty—a heavy ground-mist of the type so common in the fall of the year. Even in so quiet a spot the Boche was sure to send over an early air-patrol, and, if tanks were spotted, the whole secret would be given away. If only the mist would last, they could carry on until the safety of the wood should be reached.

At long length they reached the corner of the wood, and the crews imagined themselves to be near the end of their task. They were speedily disillusioned. It seemed that the wood stretched for nearly two miles parallel with the front line, and that it was in the farthest corner of the wood that they were to be hidden. With a weary, weary sigh, Tosh entered upon the last stage of his pilgrimage.

As they skirted the edge of the wood, which, though a mile from the line, was here almost untouched, they noticed more signs of a forth-coming attack. The wood itself was full of camps, all carefully camouflaged, while along the fringe were innumerable dumps, emplacements, and so forth. At one place was a casualty clearing station in embryo, while no fewer than three light railways ran into the wood. It was sufficiently clear that operations had been well thought out, for not a wheel-track showed in the soft mud, and Alphen explained that arrangements had been made for the tank tracks to be obliterated by the hoof-marks of the nearest horse-lines.

The ground mist was now beginning to thin, and there was some anxiety as to whether they could get in in time. Orders were given to stop and run into the wood immediately an aeroplane was heard; but no such incident occurred, and at 7.15 the tanks arrived at the section of the wood set apart for their concealment. Tosh looked about for an entry. This did not immediately offer itself, for a row of pollarded willows grew along the fringe, the difficulty being not to get in—for trees are easily pushed over—but to get in without leaving a visible gap. At last he solved the difficulty by pushing a tree over, walking over it, and then pushing it up into place again with the rear downward slope of his track.

The crews then emerged, camouflaged up, and dropped straight off to sleep in the bivvies which the advance party had already erected for them.

CHAPTER 9

Expectation

When the officers had collected for lunch some hours later, they were issued with maps of the district. They discovered themselves to be less than a mile from the front line, and only two miles from a village in Boche hands, which, the R.O. assured them, still had a few roofs on its more fortunate houses. The idea of finding a mile from the line a wood which was still a wood, a village which was still a village, or even grass which was still grass, was at first incredible, the fact being that the Boche had retreated over this ground, and had since been left in peace. The real novelty was not so much there being such a spot, as the arrival of the Tank Corps in that spot; for, being entirely concerned with offensives, it had hitherto known only such parts of the line as had already received considerable attention from the grim hand of war.

The peaceful atmosphere of this corner of the war was indescribable. By day hardly a "boom" broke the heavy silence; even by night machine-guns chattered quite perfunctorily, star-shells were few and far between, and the flash of a gun was a rare event. Meanwhile the tanks lay embowered in leafy growth, while high above them the trees met to screen them from prying eyes.

The day after the company arrived, officers and N.C.O.'s went up to the front line to have a look round. For a short distance they proceeded up a small valley, the mouth of which was hung across with camouflage. Through this screen a view could be

154

obtained of the village behind the Boche line. The R.O., who conducted the party, claimed that in one house he could even distinguish the shutters on the windows, but the village showed no sign of the troops who occupied it.

They then entered a communication-trench, cut in chalk, and beautifully revetted, with duck-boards along the bottom actually nailed down at each end. Proceeding along this, after three-quarters of a mile, they arrived at the reserve line—a system so neatly kept it appeared impossible it could be real. The troops occupying it were peacefully brewing tea; they were to be relieved before the attack, and for purposes of secrecy had not been informed of its imminence, while the tank men had been warned to give no hint.

The route to the front line was as perplexing as is usually the case, with innumerable forks and cross-routes; but before long the party arrived in the actual front line trench.

From previous experience, Tosh had been expecting to find a muddy and uncomfortable ditch, sparsely populated with weary sentries. Instead, they came into a perfect example of the traversed trench, revetted and duck-boarded, with neat shelters and bomb-stores all carefully labelled, furnished with a broad and convenient fire-step and inhabited by a number of imperturbable and immaculate Jocks, who greeted them with polite smiles and went on cleaning their rifles.

The visitors were by this time filled with amazed hilarity. But more was to come. The R.O. wished to show them the lie of the country. Instead of cautiously erecting a periscope and offering each in turn a peep he climbed on the fire-step, unconcernedly popped his head above the parapet, and invited them to come and have a look. Picture the scene, ye who have known front lines which were unsafe on hands and knees two bays full of young officers, each with a map, gazing cheerfully across direct into the Boche line! What a crime was shortly to be perpetrated in spoiling such a soldier's paradise!

No Man's Land at this point was about twelve hundred yards across, though various saps ran out from each side; it was grassy and almost untouched by fire. On the crest of a small slope could be seen the Boche wire, known to be unusually thick. Behind his front line the ground dipped to a ravine, of which only the tops of the trees lining its streamlet were visible; but beyond it rose to a well-defined ridge, on which stood a village—their final objective.

Consequently, as the front line was to be taken by another company, almost the whole of the ground they were to cover lay exposed to view; and each officer busily impressed on his memory (and on that of his N.C.O.) the actual appearance of landmarks they had already studied on the map. Having previously been issued with aeroplane-photographs of the country, they knew the ground both by front elevation and by plan!

The condition of the ground was all that could be desired; landmarks were plentiful; trenches might be wide, but were not impassable; and it was with a very definite and justifiable optimism that "C" Company looked forward to the day so nearly approaching. They were in a mood to appreciate a parapet shown them which, from the Boche side, was apparently turf, but which proved, on inspection, to be composed of 18-pdr. shells covered with sods; and to note that an old road across the front line had been stealthily repaired until it was now fit for the passage of guns and limbers.

On the return journey they passed through the scarcely discernible remains of a little village. The Boche in his retreat had blown two huge craters in the road; a new road skirted them, while the craters were used as an R.E. dump. Tosh appropriated a broom which was lying about, and gave it to his corporal to sweep out the tank with. With this small souvenir they presently arrived at the camp, and sat down to a hearty meal.

That night operation orders were issued. After the usual details regarding troops to right and left, divisional and brigade boundaries, position of dressing-stations and head-quarters, etc., detail was given of the route and objectives of each section and of each tank. On Y night, at Z—— 7 hours, the company would emerge from the wood, in order to have it free for the guns with which it was to be packed. The tanks were to wait at a point either just in advance of or just behind the front line, until Z plus 30 minutes. The first wave would by then, if all went well, have taken the front line and be attacking the support. The company would deploy into line of battle in no man's, land, where their infantry would pick them up, and the whole line would advance as detailed to the successive objectives.

A timetable of the barrage followed. As this was to be fired by calculation from unregistered guns, it would *not* be too closely followed.

There was very little comment on the orders. The major's operation orders were masterpieces of their kind, and left nothing to be explained. Each tank commander took his map and his aeroplane-photographs, retired to his bivvy, and set about making himself perfectly sure of what he had to do. Then, with hearts beating high with hope and excitement, they lay down to enjoy what might well be their last sleep for some time.

Next morning the major called a parade and addressed the company. He reminded them of their last attack and the many obstacles they had encountered—bad ground, bad weather, bad luck. Now was their chance to show that as in difficult circumstances they could stolidly fight against their difficulties, so when fortune at last turned they could make the most of a good opportunity.

Once again "C" Company had been chosen for the task which demanded enterprise and staying power; for, whereas the other companies had definite objectives, they who formed the second wave were first to overcome a series of definite obstacles, and were then to push on with an unlimited objective. He had often before spoken of "pooping off into the blue"; at last there was nothing to prevent their doing so. The whole responsibility of the attack had been deliberately thrown on the Tank Corps; it was their supreme opportunity. England expected that every tank would do its damndest.

The company having been dismissed, Tosh set about his preparations. Following his invariable rule, he destroyed all unnecessary papers, and packed his valise ready to go down the line in case of need. Having written a couple of field postcards and a letter, he cleaned and loaded his revolver, arranged his maps, packed his haversack with shaving-kit and money in case he should be wounded, filled his flask and cigarette-case, inspected his field-dressing, gave his servant instructions, and went into lunch.

The afternoon passed rapidly. Tosh first manoeuvred his fascine into fighting position. He and his crew then went over their bus, inspecting every minutest detail. Guns were prepared for action, spare water and petrol were packed where shrapnel would not harm them, ammunition was examined, and controls were tested. Finally, Tosh collected his crew and put them through a catechism as to the forthcoming operation, shortly expressed his optimism as to its result ("We'll show the —— what we're made of!"), and dismissed them to their final meal.

At 9.30 the crews paraded by sections. A few minutes were given to final instructions. At 9.45 the tanks moved out of the wood.

CHAPTER 10

The Approach-March

Approach-marches, however they may vary in detail, are inevitably similar in the emotions they arouse. Sometimes they are made over entirely unknown ground, teeming with obstacles which necessitate constant watchfulness. Sometimes they involve miles of driving along a narrow sleeper-road packed with excited horse-transport, while on either side a yawning ditch awaits the unlucky. Sometimes, as in the present case, they consist merely in cautious and silent driving over previously reconnoitred ground. Occasionally they are made amid the continuous crash of shells and blast of guns; more usually they are made in a waiting hush when every sound appears a betrayal. But, vary the details as you like, the heart of the matter remains the same—a breathless anxiety, a desperate hope, and a heartfelt wish to throw off the mask and be at them at last.

As the tanks swung into line, Tosh, whose place was fifth, looked back at those who followed him. In this supreme hour of secrecy, not the glimmer of a torch might be shown, and tank commanders must strain their eyes in the dark and see as best they might. But in front of every tank was a glowing point of light every pilot was smoking, and with his cigarette could signal to his crew. The irresistibly animal appearance of the tanks was greatly heightened as they loomed ghostly out of the darkness; used as he was to the sight, Tosh was tempted to pat his beast on the track as it lumbered faithfully after him.

After half an hour's slow running, the tanks swung across a

road. Like every other road on that fateful night, it was a solid mass of slow-moving traffic. The thousands of empty gun-emplacements would not still be empty at zero! As they went forward the night was stealthily alive with chinks of harness and rumble of wheels, and everywhere they passed groups of men busy with mysterious activities. Occasionally a star-shell floated in the distant air, its light revealing that the country was full of men and horses; then darkness closed down again, and only their stealthy noises betrayed their presence.

As the line advanced, the occasional chatter of machine-guns began to sound very close. Soon they were carefully negotiating the reserve-line, and all about them were infantry advancing across the open. Suddenly there came a disturbance away to the left. Trench-mortars barked viciously, machine-guns took up the affray, and five-nines might be heard whining across, to crump methodically in the little village away to the left. What did it mean? Had the Boche heard? Did he suspect, or was it merely a case of nerves? For some minutes the noise continued, then gradually died down and all was silence.

Presently the tanks in front of Tosh stopped, and he went forward to discover the reason. It appeared that it still wanted an hour to zero, and they had almost arrived at the front line. As they were sheltered here by rising ground, the major had determined to wait for half an hour before proceeding. Tosh stopped his engine, and explained the matter to his crew, who gladly came out of their stuffy steel box for fresh air and quiet. Tosh thereupon rejoined the officers .

Here a discussion was proceeding. It will be remembered that from zero to Z, plus 30, the company was to lie up near the front line, the discussion being whether they should halt just behind the front line or push forward into no man's land. Amid all the uncertainty of the immediate future, one thing was certain—our barrage at zero would provoke some sort of a counter-barrage. Now in the old days such a counter-barrage was usually laid on and behind the front line; but of late, with the increase in width of no man's land, a custom had grown up

160

of barraging that debatable ground itself. After some talk it was decided to halt immediately behind the front line.

The half hour passed, but slowly. The night had grown bitterly cold, and all ranks were too much occupied with their own thoughts to indulge in light conversation. Tosh, for one, was heartily glad when the signal came to go on.

The trail now passed over a number of jumps. Tosh for the first time remembered the ton of wood balancing above his head, and how frail was its supporting hook. Consequently, it seemed to him a short interval indeed before they again halted, and his watch showed the time to be twenty minutes before zero. Indeed, the night was no longer dark; already a pale glow showed in the east, and it was with an uncomfortable sense of visibility that he sought company for the last dreary wait.

It is a truism that the best way to overcome nervousness is to make a joke of it. To this may be directly traced that traditional spirit of careless mockery which, in spite of the stress laid upon it by newspaper correspondents, was in very truth the outstanding feature of the armies in France. In the present case, there was no question of the concealment of fear—everyone there, from long experience, knew that his companions were experiencing the same symptoms, and was much too sure of himself to suppose that they indicated fear.

But set the least imaginative of men in their position, a few yards from an enemy with whom in five minutes he will be engaged in a desperate struggle for life, and whether he be brave man or coward, or that wonderful mean which this war has shown is so gloriously common, he must feel some warning of overstrung nerves. Consequently as the officers sat round the rim of a shell-hole, they busied themselves with humorous descriptions of their own feelings, interspersed with gleeful pictures of the state of unpreparedness of the enemy, and the awful surprise which awaited him.

So passed ten minutes. It was now Z-10, and rising with one accord, they went forward beyond the tanks and peered into no man's land. Somewhere ahead in battle array, "A" and "B" Company awaited the signal which for them would be the beginning of the attack. In the grey dawn, the further ridge was just visible, but no tanks or infantry could be distinguished. Slowly, in ticks which might have been heart-beats, the seconds passed; five minutes to go, four minutes, three minutes, two minutes—a long breath.

"Now for it," cried the major.

With the words, as at some dread command, the silence was rent with stupendous clamour, as up and down the line for miles thousands of guns belched flame. With a cataclysmic crash the Boche line erupted in spouting volcanoes of smoke and earth, illumined in the flickering light of the incessant bursts. A second or two, and right, left and centre, up went flares of all colours—red, green, yellow, singly and in clusters—as the terrified front-line troops called upon their artillery to save them from annihilation. Meanwhile the officers, released at last from the intolerable strain of silence, cried out in delighted profanity at the hellish din of the barrage. No one could hear his neighbour's voice—the field-guns were seeing to that—all were perfectly happy to shout their comments to the air.

As the excitement gradually died down, they strained their eyes to see how their friends had been faring. Dawn was breaking, but the dust of the barrage and a thin ground-mist hid all sight of the enemy lines. Returning to their buses, the crews awaited, amid the crashing thunder, the signal to take their part in the fray.

CHAPTER 11

Realization

Compared with the half hour before zero, the half hour after zero passed in a flash, and Tosh seemed hardly to have reached his seat before the line was in motion, and he found himself carefully crossing the British front line.

In no man's land the tanks were to adopt battle formation; but to avoid loss of direction (the bugbear of advancing troops) they first divided into left and right half companies, and continued to advance in column of route. The left half company, of which Tosh was the centre, followed an old road to where it forked, and, avoiding the huge crater which the Boche had blown on his retirement, they spread out fan wise until, the centre pair waiting for the flanks to take position, the half company was in line of battle.

The right flank was now in touch with the left flank of the right half company, and with slight readjustments of distance the whole line advanced to the first trench in parade formation. The subsequent five minutes were to Tosh a very anxious time. The front and support lines should by this time have been taken, but manifold are the unexpected chances of war, and at any moment he might be greeted with a hail of bullets. Meanwhile, as he crackled merrily through the wire, he was forced to slow down to keep his place in the line.

At last the front line came into view, a huge trench whose difficulties had not been overestimated . Captured obviously, and in our hands; but where were the flags which were to have marked the presence of the first wave's fascines? Anxiously Tosh peered right and left. No sign of a flag; but away to the right he saw the explanation.

Three tanks were ditched there, close together. Either their fascines had fallen off or they had proved useless, and the attempt to cross without had failed. Tosh determined to drop his own fascine. Lifting his hand to the lever he pulled it to one side; with a crackle the great bundle lurched forward, and dropped accurately into the trench. Tosh signalled his driver to go forward; the tank's nose dropped true on to the fascine, and in a second they were across. A glance behind showed that the nearest tank was preparing to follow him across.

By this slight failure in the plans, Tosh was prepared to find part of the support line in enemy possession, and advanced with every nerve strained. Such did not prove entirely the case, for soon he could see Jocks in the trench; but, as he approached them, they pointed wildly in a slightly left direction. As Tosh looked that way, suddenly with a tremendous thwack a bullet struck an inch from the open flap and scattered red-hot chips over his face. With hasty hand he closed the shutter, and peered about through a periscope to locate the aggressor. Meanwhile the solitary shot was followed by a shower which played a regular devil's tattoo within a foot of Tosh's nose.

The noise made by the impact of a bullet on a tank is unlike any other—a peculiar, ringing thwack, which is always associated with the smell of burnt paint. Such bullets as strike near a flap or gun-port send in a shower of red-hot chips which are apt to lodge under the skin of the tank commander, whence, if left alone, they emerge a few weeks later. The phenomenon of the speckled face is one familiar to all who have seen tank crews after action.

Tosh, in the present case, received a few chips, but soon covered his face with his tin hat; and, while his hands were stinging under the shower they were receiving, he succeeded in spotting the source of these unwelcome attentions—a concrete pill-box almost hidden under tree-trunks and rubble. From previous experience, he expected a stout resistance, but the enemy were too badly shaken, and at the second well-placed shot from the port six-pounder the firing ceased and the garrison surrendered. Leaving them to the care of the infantry, Tosh went on his way rejoicing. All anxiety, as usual, had vanished at the sound of his own gun, leaving only a burning impatience to get on.

In crossing the front and support lines, the tanks had necessarily lost their dressing, but, none having been ditched, distances were soon corrected, and the laggards drew level. The co-operating infantry appeared as if by magic, and the second phase of the operation commenced. Unfortunately, however, time had been lost, and they were a good half-hour behind the barrage.

The first objective was a small switch-line running out at an angle to the reserve system. This, it had been anticipated, would prove a tough obstacle. But the sudden onset out of the dark of innumerable prehistoric monsters had considerably upset the enemy, and beyond occasional fugitives from earlier objectives the trench was deserted.

As has been mentioned, it ran at an angle to the previous lines. As the smoke-barrage had entirely obscured the distant landmarks, there was a tendency among the advancing Tanks to lose direction. Tosh easily surmounted this difficulty. His orders were to strike a road running up the slope and follow it; this he proceeded to do.

The wave of tanks now approached a railway cutting. This had been utilized by the enemy, not as a line of defence, but as a system of suburban residences. Nevertheless, as the tanks came up they were greeted with a fair sprinkling of bullets. At a later date there were conflicting claims among the crews regarding the share of each in the demolishment of these machine-guns; at the moment all Tosh observed was that his starboard gun fired three rounds, while, as they crossed the cutting, he saw an involved medley of steel and flesh which had recently been a machine-gun and crew.

But better things were in store for Tank 2597. In accordance with orders, she pushed straight on to the next objective, while her companions to right and left remained to assist the infantry in clearing dugouts. She was then in a position to make good use of any opportunities which might offer.

Tosh soon arrived at his mark, a long zig-zag trench running right across from a village well to the left of the company front to the village which formed their final objective. At the point where he crossed, it was empty, but, as he swung to patrol along it, suddenly, away to the left, he saw grey-clad figures leap from shelter and run wildly right across his front.

Then for the crew of Tank 2597 began the rabbit-shooting of their fondest dreams. Streams and streams of the enemy, their retreat cut off by Tosh and their front menaced by the approaching wave, broke wildly from cover. As fast as the gunners could reload, they poured in a hail of bullets, Tosh himself firing and yelling like a maniac. At last the panic subsided, the remainder of the enemy apparently realizing the futility of an attempt to escape; but it left Tosh and his crew hoarse with joy and almost beside themselves with excitement. To those who have never experienced it, the lust of battle must always appear unnatural and terrible; but ever after Tosh would look back to those few minutes of slaughter as among the most joyful moments of his life.

With the cessation of the panic bolt, all appeared to be over, and Tosh proceeded slowly parallel with the trench. Suddenly, in a shell-hole dead ahead, he noticed three living figures—Boche—in grey uniforms and big black helmets, *kamerading*. He drew closer to within a few yards. His approach threw them into the last extremity of terror; faces mottled with sickly green, eyes starting, mouths agape, their bodies racked with trembling, they knew not whether to bolt and be shot or stay and be run over.

Tosh too was faced with a problem. If he left them they would infallibly get away to the enemy lines, but to shoot them in cold blood did not appeal to his instincts. Finally he swung left and blotted them from his mind.

He was now approaching another section of the trench he had crossed. To his astonishment he found it still full of Boches, about 150 with two officers, all *kamerading* in approved style, and throwing equipment bombs and rifles on to the parapet. This was too much for a man in Tosh's state of excitement. In defiance of orders, armed only with a revolver, he climbed out of his tank and strolled up and down the parados, yelling at the dumbfounded enemy in a marvellous mixture of bad French and worse Dutch, until finally the infantry arrived at the double, and he handed over the prisoners, climbed into the bus and carried on with the war.

Up till now the operation had progressed with a smoothness rarely seen in war. Two miles and a half of enemy territory had been stormed at an insignificant cost, and there seemed nothing to prevent a like further advance. But it is behind her broadest smile that Fortune ever hides her most dastardly plots.

The last objective to be tackled was the support system, which was as strong as the front line system, and had had due warning of attack. It lay over the crest of the slope up which the Tanks had been working, and was thus still out of sight. Tosh's first duty was to inspect a cemetery slightly in advance of the line. This proved to have been abandoned; but the time taken to examine it had sufficed for the infantry to occupy the front line of the new system.

As Tosh crawled over the crest of the rise and crossed the trench, he noticed several Jocks pointing ahead and waving their arms wildly. He peered out, but could see no reason for their warning. As he was following the safe procedure of peppering all the surrounding country with his machine-gun, his attention was caught and held by an appalling sight. A tank to the right had suddenly burst into a bright sheet of flame, while such of the crew as were able could be seen scuttling like rabbits to shelter. A premonition passed through his mind—field-guns! He turned back to try and spot them, when suddenly, at his very ear, there came a bang like unto the crack of doom, and all round him was flame and choking vapour, and the awful screaming of stricken men.

In subsequent recollection only two impressions remained

of the next few seconds. He could remember crying "Get out of it," at the top of his voice, and he could remember a terrible second while scrambling, scrabbling men tried to open the side door. When next his mind could record impressions he was lying flat in a shallow trench twenty yards away, his first driver by his side.

Tosh himself and the first driver were uninjured. Close by, in the trench, Tosh saw his N.C.O., who proved to be unhurt save for a generous lump of metal in the right cheek. He reported that the third driver, apparently demented, had fled wildly to the cemetery, fifty yards away. Of the eight, therefore, four were almost untouched.

The air was now fairly alive with bullets, but Tosh and his men, bent almost double, gained the partial shelter of the burning tank. Here they found a gunner, his face yellow with lyddite and distorted with shock. On examination, he had nothing worse than a broken leg and a slight arm-wound, but at present he was too dazed to help himself. They carried him to the comparative safety of the trench and returned to the tank. They then discovered a second gunner, evidently too far gone for help. He showed small signs of any wound, but even as Tosh bent over him he straightened slowly, spread his arms, and with a half-sigh he was dead.

"Poor old Jimmie," said the first driver, "he never knew what hit him."

Tosh turned his head away towards the tank, started, and clutched his driver's arm. From the open door of what was now a smoking ruin crawled a terrible figure. One arm was smashed to pulp, one leg dragged; the body was soaked in blood. But the face—one whole cheek had been blown away, and through the gaping hole the tongue could be seen working feverishly over the shattered jaw. Worse still, the light in the eyes left no room for merciful doubt but that the wreck of a man was still sane. There was no shadow of pain—Tosh seized that crumb of comfort—only a strained perplexity at the unwieldiness of the crippled body.

Fighting with the deadly nausea which almost choked him, Tosh went to the man—his best gunner and firmest friend—and took him in his arms. After a moment's inspection he reached for his revolver, and for twenty seconds tried to nerve himself to the merciful deed. But the decision was too hard for him. Ghastly as the man's wounds were, he might not be beyond hope, and for the moment he could not—his eyes showed that he could not be suffering. With a sob Tosh laid him down and turned away.

The tank was burning fiercely, and the exploding ammunition made a continuous rattle. One man was still unaccounted for; but to enter her was impossible, and nothing could still be alive in that inferno. Beyond his revolver Tosh had no weapon. His first duty, therefore, was towards his wounded.

With many a stumble and many a rest in shell-holes, the three unwounded men carried off the gunner with the broken leg. The air was still full of the clack and whine of bullets, while the field gun which had knocked Tosh out was sending shells so low as apparently to skim the ground. Making for the cemetery they kept behind the shelter of its little quickset hedge, in which birds still twittered, and so, stumbling among the tombstones, came at last to the sunken cross-road behind it, where they deposited their burden.

Leaving the two men to tie up their comrade, Tosh set about discovering the whereabouts of his section commander, who had been in the tank on his right. The first available Jock informed him that a captain of the tanks, who had been blown up, was sitting "ben" in the trench a little to the right. Tosh immediately set off in that direction; but he must have carried in his face potent signs of the events of the last half-hour, for his informant set off with him, and, questions, entreaties and commands notwithstanding, insisted on following him wherever he went.

Thus personally conducted, Tosh entered the trench where it opened on the sunken road, and, while bullets clacked merrily overhead, pushed past the kilted occupants until he came upon his skipper.

Captain Alphen, M.C., was seated on the fire-step talking to Herr Von, in whose tank he had been accommodated. Both were busily engaged in eating chocolate. As Tosh came round the traverse, they greeted him with a cheery hail and offered him a slab. They, too, it seemed, had been knocked out, but without serious casualties, and had taken refuge in this, the nearest trench. Tosh accepted the chocolate, and gave half to his faithful Jock, who made his *adieux* with a broad smile on his honest face.

With the opportunity to tell his experiences Tosh felt relief from the load of horror which had oppressed him; and such is the elasticity of the human spirit that soon he was laughing with them at the dramatic change in the situation.

"Well, anyway," said Alphen, "none of us are in a position to do anything. The infantry have had no casualties worth speaking of, and have the situation well in hand. Come along, Tosh, and we'll see about your wounded. Herr Von, collect your crew and take them off to the rendezvous in the railway cutting. I'll be along there presently."

On arriving at the sunken cross-roads, they found the gunner with the broken leg recovered from his shock, and he was despatched to the dressing station leaning on the shoulder of the corporal, whose face now obviously needed attention. The gunner who had bolted at the time of the explosion had now returned, and shamefacedly reported to Tosh; he had lost three fingers of his right hand, and nine-tenths of his nerve, and was sent off down the road after the others. Finally, the first driver was entrusted with a message to the major at the rendezvous.

Having disposed of the walking wounded, Tosh turned his attention to bringing back the only remaining number of the crew. Stretcher-bearers were few and far between, but he succeeded in finding two. These he conducted through the cemetery, which still hummed with bullets, and between them they brought the pitiful wreck of a man to the cross-road. Tosh noted with a sigh of relief that he was now delirious.

The next requisite was a stretcher. Prospecting along the road, Tosh found a Boche officer with a shattered leg lying on one waiting to be carried down. This was no time for niceties of behaviour. Lifting off the protesting man, they seized the stretcher, and in a minute Tosh was supporting his driver while the stretcher-bearers raised the load on to their shoulders.

The way to the dressing-station lay along a road, but it was long and very tiring for the bearers. To Tosh it was endless, for the delirious man kept making determined efforts to get off the stretcher, groaning and crying the while with pain and mumbling and mowing with his shattered jaws. At last they reached the dressing-station, where the doctor pronounced the case very serious, but not altogether hopeless.

Tosh now proceeded to the rendezvous. Here he was met with the news of the death of the major five minutes after the beginning of the attack. The second in command, now acting O.C., ordered all crews of knocked-out tanks to report themselves at the camp in the wood. Weary to death, but cheerful, they lightened the way with the swapping of experiences, and at last in utter fatigue Tosh crept into bed and fell into dreamless sleep.

CHAPTER 12

The Price

Next morning Tosh permitted himself the luxury of breakfast in bed. In spite of some gruesome memories, his prevailing feeling was of intense satisfaction. The corps had broken a famous trench-system; the company had lived up to its reputation; he himself had shot many Boches and had escaped death by a miracle.

The morning was fully occupied in making out reports. Every subaltern in the Tank Corps enjoys after action the doubtful privilege of writing a detailed history of his performance, together with any suggestions he may wish to make regarding future shows. This *Battle History Sheet* is forwarded to Corps H.Q., and in some cases to G.H.Q. itself. Its composition frequently causes more misgivings than the action it is intended to describe.

At lunch Alphen informed Tosh that, as the line was now two miles beyond the cemetery, a burial party would be going up that afternoon. Tosh decided to accompany it, if only to make certain of the fate of his seventh man—reported killed.

At two o'clock the party fell in and were marched off. At first they followed the tank-track of two nights ago, but under slightly different circumstances. What had been a silent waste where men went delicately was now a caravanserai of horse-lines, camps, and battery positions. Already the grass had been trampled into mud a foot deep, and for any attempt at camouflage the Boche might have been a hundred miles off instead of five.

Skirting the craters on the road, they passed through the ruined village and so across no man's land of yesterday to the old Boche front line. Occasional "stiffs" were to be seen lying about, already swollen and fly-covered, but nothing had been left which might furnish a souvenir. Equipment, badges, great-coats, all had been taken—the Jocks had been here!

Down in the ravine they came on the surviving tanks of the company, under guard, and halted while Alphen gave a few instructions. They then climbed the further slope, past the railway cutting, in which Jocks were now accommodated, and came to the trench which had provided Tosh with so much sport. The evidences of that sport were lying about, and he realized with something of a shock that these had been fellow-men he had so delighted to shoot.

The party now arrived at the cemetery, and fell out for five minutes before commencing their unpleasant task. From where Tosh sat he looked away across open country to a village beneath a wooded crest. Here lay the present front line, but no sound gave evidence of the armed forces concealed in that blue expanse. The air, however, was full of the hum of aeroplanes, and high overhead passed a squadron going up to reconnoitre.

The five minutes up, Alphen took half the men off to the right, while with the other half Tosh sought his own tank.

As they drew near they came first upon the dead gunner. Arms outstretched, eyes staring at the sky, on his face a complete negation of expression, he seemed to Tosh a poignant reminder of the vanity of the flesh, and a potent indication of the spirit's immortality. These men with him—they had known the dead so much better than he—did they not feel the impossibility of this clay being all that was left of their friend and companion?

Leaving his men to dig the grave and compose the body, Tosh passed to the farther side of the tank. From this side had come the shells. As he looked at that battered, broken wreck, he marvelled that anyone had come out of it alive. Seven shells in all had entered, and the shape was almost unrecognisable. Drawing

173

nearer, Tosh peered in, and was left in no further doubt of the fate of his seventh man.

Stepping back from the stench, he called for four men and a blanket.

"My God," said one, "burnt to death."

"No, you fool," exclaimed Tosh, with a queer irritability, "can't you see he was killed before he was burnt? Come on, let's get it over."

In the pitiful blanket shroud the body was carried to the grave. Setting up the cross they had brought, the men covered it in; Tosh nailed on the two name-plates; together they saluted the dead and passed on.

The next tank to be dealt with lay to the left. On their way to it they passed a point where fighting had been more severe, and all about lay bodies. For the sake of the mothers to whom he must shortly write, Tosh was glad that the Tank Corps usually found opportunity to bury its own dead within a few days of battle.

Arrived at the tank the men were faced with a particularly horrible work. A shell had landed on the cab, killing instantaneously both officer and first driver, and a fire subsequently starting, the bodies had been roasted where they lay. The officer had been a particular friend of Tosh's—still a boy at heart, with a boy's gaiety and untainted outlook on life. The death of a friend he had grown used to, but this was no ordinary death. Sick at heart, he thanked God that he directed but need bear no actual hand.

The burial finished, Tosh threw off his haunting visions and marched off the men to rejoin Captain Alphen's party. Together they then marched through the village which the day before had formed their final objective. Only one tank had penetrated the village; towards her their steps were now bent.

It was on the very extremity of the village that they came upon her. In the field beyond three field-guns still lay. Having been warned of her approach, they had evidently watched for her appearance, and no sooner had she cleared the last house than they had reduced her to a flaming hulk.

Of her crew of eight, four had escaped and had crept back through the enemy lines to safety. The other four were known by name, but their bodies were quite unrecognisable.

On the way home that night, Tosh marvelled at his insensibility. He and his men had seen sights that day which might have haunted them for life. Yet here they were, within an hour, joking with one another, looking forward to a hearty supper and a dreamless night's sleep. Yet they were not hardened or callous—at heart he knew them to be sympathetic almost to a fault.

On arrival in the camp it was announced that next afternoon all effectives would move forward to billets four miles in advance.

CHAPTER 13

Orchestra Stalls

Details of the move were to hand next morning. The infantry, it seemed, had struck a tough proposition on ahead, and tomorrow a full-dress tank attack was to be made on it. The orders were to continue attacking until it was taken; consequently reinforcements for the crews must be on the spot to replace casualties. All crews still complete with tanks would move up in the evening and attack next day; those who had succeeded in getting rid of their charges would be spectators of the battle unless, and until, their services should be required. As on many previous occasions, Tosh congratulated himself on his facility in that most highly-prized of tank arts—the art of leaving your bus on the field of battle!

The "non-combatants," as the acting O.C. described them, paraded at 3 p.m. Tosh had carefully packed his valise and handed it over to the camp guard; on his shoulders he carried his immediate necessities for the ensuing week.

They proceeded first to Herr Von's derelict tank. It had been effectively knocked out. but had not caught fire. Tosh left his party to transfer ammunition from it to such mobile buses as needed it, while he strolled off to examine the battery which had knocked him out, whence he shortly returned with an electric torch and an aluminium drinking-flask. Considering that the Jocks had been before him, he was satisfied even with so poor a haul.

The light was now failing, and it devolved upon Tosh to go

ahead and find a route for the tanks. This proved simple enough; but it provided him with a sensation he was never to forget— the feeling of having "broken through" the trench system to "the blue" that lay beyond. Later on, both sides would grow well acquainted with that feeling, but at the time it was as rare as it was blissful.

After a three-mile drive the company arrived at the little village where the tanks were to lie up for the night. At the time of their arrival the place was quiet and seemingly deserted, though it lay only 800 yards behind the front line. A billet having been found for the men, and a fire started for their dixies, the officers discovered a house with its roof intact, and were soon enjoying a hot meal.

The guns that night were quiet, being engaged in preparation for the morrow. But sooner or later the village was bound to come under heavy shell-fire, for the enemy had hurried up reserves and would not easily relinquish the position to be stormed. It was therefore decided not to sleep in the village, but to move to a line of dugouts some five hundred yards back. A wise decision without doubt; but unfortunately other people had arrived at the same conclusion, and when Tosh finally settled down it was in a dugout with thirty men of a signalling section, on a wire bed none too broad with three bed-fellows to keep him snug. It is not often that the Tank Corps is compelled to sleep in dugouts; this was a Boche dugout and contained a liberal supply of voracious fauna; the air was stuffy in the extreme; yet Tosh slept like a lamb until seven next morning.

On waking he rose, stretched himself, staggered up the ninety steps of the dugout and stood at the top gulping the fresh morning air. Near at hand he discovered the mess servants serving breakfast—a most welcome sight.

Zero that morning had been fixed for the unusual hour of ten. Tosh discovered that the acting company commander was going up on foot behind the attacking wave to see how things progressed, and succeeded in being allowed to go with him. More Pilkinson refused to take, and the reader will be well advised if he follows the example of the scribe and remains at a safe distance from the imminent battle.

From the line of dugouts in which they had slept, the little party of "non-combatants" obtained such a view of the battlefield as is usually vouchsafed only to "balloonatics" or war correspondents. From where they sat the ground sloped gently to a hollow in which lay the village. Here the tanks were parked; while near them lay several batteries of field guns, rushed up the night before. At the moment they were covered up and deserted, but doubtless in the fullness of time their crews would appear.

Beyond the village the ground rose evenly again to the wood-crowned ridge some two miles off. Somewhere on that slope was the front line, while the wood was today's final objective. It was known to be packed full of machine-guns in the hands of desperate crews, yet in the morning light it lay peaceful and apparently deserted.

At nine the tanks moved off in file, skirted the village, and were lost to sight in the valley. At 9.15 a Boche battery began shelling the village. The whines and crashes came in regular succession, raising clouds of red brick-dust, but no shells came near the dugouts. At 9.30 there were signs of activity among the batteries in the hollow. Guns were uncovered and swung into position, while signallers could be seen selecting points of observation.

Aeroplanes now began to arrive, patrol by patrol, till the air was full of the hum of their engines. In the interest of a contest between six British and nine enemy 'planes, the spectators forgot to watch the time, and it was the sudden crash of the artillery in the valley which apprised them of the fact that the battle had begun.

To men who three days before had been in the thick of a similar affair, the panorama-view of that day's attack was an unforgettable experience. The first thing to strike them was the noise. To the men actually engaged, the noise of modern war is an incidental hardly worthy of note; but in the position they were now in the crews were astonished at the din even of so ragged a barrage as was put up that day. Yet through all the thunder of the guns, the wicked chattering of innumerable machine-guns beat upon the ear in a vast wave of sound. "My God," said Tosh's first driver "what a hell of a hot shop it must be!"

For at least an hour nothing could be seen of the actual attack. A copious smoke barrage enveloped the ridge, while the lower slope was invisible. The spectators therefore turned their attention to a battery close by. The battery commander could be seen signalling the various lifts of the barrage, the signals being repeated at each gun, while the stripped crews sweated and strained to get off the maximum number of rounds. In the distance a flag-signaller was sending what seemed like an endless succession of O.K.'s.

In the air, too, there was plenty to engage attention. Patrols of low-flying aeroplanes wheeled constantly over the village, dashing to the lines and dipping down with their tip-tilted tails exactly as a dragon-fly dips to the water. As one such patrol wheeled in line, suddenly the rear machine swerved sideways and down, and, quick as light, it was a flaming wreck beside the village.

Meanwhile, high in the upper levels the spotters and the fighters were at work, guns spitting viciously as foe met foe. A Boche which had broken through came directly overhead, the crosses on her wings plainly discernible, and, as she wheeled over the batteries, dropped a long streamer of black smoke. For a full half-hour the crews expected the answering salvo, but none came, and the enemy were content to paste the village methodically with five-nines.

The smoke barrage being now over, in a few minutes some of the tanks were visible half-way up the ridge. "C" Company was working close to the wood, and nothing could be seen of them but the irregular flashes of their six-pounders; but away to the left —— Battalion could clearly be seen cresting the slope. One, as it topped the hill, appeared for a few seconds to have stopped; then suddenly came a flash, and a column of smoke mingled with vicious stabs of flame.

"Knocked out," exclaimed someone, "wonder who the poor blighters are!"

All there knew from the most recent experience what it meant to be knocked out!

The attack had now been in full swing for two hours, a time which the staff had judged amply sufficient for the taking of all objectives. Consequently the barrage abruptly ceased: the batteries covered up; and the gunners presumably attacked their lunch. Yet the machine-gun fire had not diminished the slightest degree in intensity, and from a good five hundred yards *behind* the guns it could be seen that the wood was not by any means captured. The Tank Corps is too well used to ignorant criticism to indulge in it to any unreasonable extent, but with the thought of what their comrades were going through many curses were poured out on the heedless heads of the R.F.A.

The crews were seated on the bank of a main road. Along this road presently came a little group of walking wounded. To eager questions they would answer but little. Yes, the machine-gun fire was hellish, but there was no shelling to speak of. Couldn't say how the attack was going—seemed to be all right. How far was the C.C.S.? Oh, yes, a Blighty all right, but damn painful at present. Had they any water to give away?

After continuing for four hours the firing seemed now to be slackening. Gradually it petered out and all was silence. The flashes of six-pounders could no longer be seen, while the Tanks on the left had disappeared. Soon down the slope to the left of the village there came into view first one, then another, then two more, till finally—praises be!—the total number which had gone in were in sight. Their troubles were not entirely over, for the Boche had them under observation, and was sniping them with five-nines; but they did not tarry on the homeward journey, and sniping with a five-nine at a moving target is no easy matter.

A couple of eager spirits dashed off to get the first news. But Tosh's driver had his eye on two men who were approaching along the road. One, to all appearance an officer, had his arm in a sling, while the other was carrying two kits.

"By ——, it's him," ejaculated the first driver. "Look here, sir," he said to Herr Von, "here comes Mr. —— along the road. Looks as if he's stopped something."

As the pair came near, there could be no doubt of their identity. Hayles, the orderly, looked relieved on seeing his friends, but on Tosh's face was such a medley of amusement, shame and rejoicing as moved Herr Von to most unsympathetic laughter.

"Well, you old humbug," he called, "don't tell me you've been getting hurt? Were you opening a tin of bully, or what? Seriously, though, it's not bad, is it?"

"Hell, no," replied Tosh, "only an in-and-out. But, my oath, I've never been so surprised in my life. There were the three of us, Pilkinson, Hayles and I, sitting as cushy as you like in a shell-hole miles away from everything, when all of a sudden—ping! ping! wheesh!, and here was me with a ruddy wound! Easy as kiss my hand

"The show? Bit of a washout, I'm afraid. You see, the wood's too thick for tanks, and no matter how far we went along the edge the infantry couldn't stand the flanking fire. The place was lousy with machine-guns, and most of our buses got casualties from them. We must have killed off any number of Boches, though. Simpson and Dolph got right into the village behind the wood, but the infantry couldn't hold more than half the slope, so we left them there in an old Boche trench.

"You know when I think of those poor blighters in the buses, going through hell and having nothing to show for it, and me sitting watching, to go and get a cushy one!

"However, a joke's a joke, but this thing is getting stiff, and I don't want any tetanus, so I'll push off. Come on, Hayles, you come along with me. Well, see you chaps in a month's time, I expect. Meanwhile, hospital, sheets, and a V.A.D.! Cheerioh!"

And, to a chorus of "Cheeriohs" and "Good lucks," he turned his back on the tanks and walked off down the road.

Lightning Source UK Ltd.
Milton Keynes UK
UKOW051519020212

186541UK00001B/153/P